The Medical Transcription Career Handbook

The Medical Transcription Career Handbook

Keith A. Drake

Prentice Hall Health
Upper Saddle River, NJ 07458

Library of Congress Cataloging-in-Publication Data

Drake, Keith A.
    Medical transcription career handbook / Keith A. Drake.
      p.   cm.
    Includes bibliographical references and index.
    ISBN 0-13-011540-1 (pbk. : alk. paper)
    1. Medical transcription—Vocational guidance.   I. Title.
R728.8.D73   1999
653'.18—dc21   99-37072
                                         CIP

Publisher: *Julie Alexander*
Editor-in-Chief: *Cheryl Mehalik*
Acquisitions Editor: *Mark Cohen*
Editorial Assistant: *Melissa Kerian*
Director of Marketing: *Leslie Cavaliere*
Marketing Manager: *Tiffany Price*
Marketing Coordinator: *Cindy Frederick*
Director of Production and Manufacturing: *Bruce Johnson*
Managing Production Editor: *Patrick Walsh*
Production Liaison: *Cathy O'Connell*
Production Editor: *Susan Geraghty*
Senior Production Manager: *Ilene Sanford*
Creative Director: *Marianne Frasco*
Cover Design: *Bruce Kenselaar*
Composition: *Circle Graphics*
Presswork/Binding: *R.R. Donnelley & Sons, Harrisonburg, VA*

10 9 8 7 6 5 4 3 2

ISBN 0-13-011540-1

Prentice-Hall International (UK) Limited, *London*
Prentice-Hall of Australia Pty. Limited, *Sydney*
Prentice-Hall Canada Inc., *Toronto*
Prentice-Hall Hispanoamericana, S.A. *Mexico*
Prentice-Hall of India Private Limited, *New Delhi*
Prentice-Hall of Japan, Inc., *Tokyo*
Prentice-Hall (Singapore) Pte. Ltd.
Editora Prentice-Hall do Brasil, Ltda, *Rio de Janeiro*

Contents

Acknowledgments

In any large, complex project, many hands contribute to producing the whole. This book has been greatly enhanced by the talents of my contributors: Cynthia Lewis, Penny Nicholls Mann, Susan K. Hamlin, Renee Priest, Bronwen Taylor, Marcy Diehl, Mark Aguirre, Hazel Tank, Claudia Tessier of the American Association for Medical Transcription, Peggy Donaldson, Mary Morken, and Edward S. Rosenthal, CEO of Next Generation Technologies, Inc.

My thanks go also to my wife, Kate, for working extra shifts to allow me the time and financial support to write this book.

Additionally, I give great credit to my editor, Mark Cohen, for supplying the concept, the opportunity, and the encouragement to make this handbook happen, and to my copyeditor, Bruce Crabtree, for his excellent work. Finally, a special thanks to the following reviewers who critiqued my manuscript during the developmental stages of this book.

Charlene Almendarez, CMT
Program Director, Medical Transcription
Gateway Community College

Florence C. Maloney, Ed.D
Professor Emeritus, CUNY

Readers may e-mail the author at <ekard@aol.com>.

1
Becoming a Medical Transcriptionist

LEARNING OBJECTIVES

- List three qualifications for becoming a medical transcriptionist
- Describe several elements of a transcription training program
- Explain the value of participating in aptitude testing before selecting the transcription profession
- Discuss ways to analyze the local job market for transcription positions

 ON-THE-JOB PROFILE

The "Accidental" Transcriptionist

Although I've had a lifelong interest in health care, my own entry into medical transcription, in 1985, was unplanned. I had a good medical background, having been trained as a hospital ward clerk in the 1970s. I had also attended graduate school in library science, and I managed a small medical library for two years. So I knew some medical terminology and was familiar with basic lab tests and hospital procedures.

By 1985 I was working in an architectural library in Austin, Texas. Somehow I managed to quit that job just as Texas was falling into a terrible recession. When I began seeking another library position, I discovered that no one was hiring. In fact, for one of the jobs I applied there had been 210 applicants!

Lacking a regular, "permanent" position, I went to a temporary employment company. They interviewed me and reviewed my resume. Then the examiner said, "You have some good medical experience from your job in that library. Can you type?"

"Of course," I said. "I'm also a writer."

"Well," the examiner continued, "we rarely get anything in library science. But if you could do medical transcription, I could start you working tomorrow!"

"What's transcription?" I asked.

ON-THE-JOB PROFILE   (continued)

The examiner took me over to a work-station with a typewriter and a transcriber. She showed me how to operate the transcriber and the foot pedal and let me practice with it. It seemed a long way away from cataloging books, but I could do it and I needed a job.

Within a day or two I was working temporarily at a family practice office connected with a major medical center. They had me using one of the new "electronic" typewriters, which I really enjoyed compared to the manual Underwood I had learned on. Luckily the work was not difficult—mostly clinic notes. After four weeks I heard of a permanent position available in the hospital, in radiology. They hired me, and a new career had begun. My medical library background had given me just enough knowledge to begin learning the massive lexicon of the medical transcriptionist.

I sometimes thought of returning to my chosen profession, but there was always so much work to be done in transcription. In 14 years I can only remember a few days with work slowdowns. Usually the backlog at my job is so high I can work as much as I want part-time, full-time, or more! In my current position with a university hospital, I have staff ID and educational benefits, which helps me feel included in the academic community.

The knowledge and skills needed by a multispecialty medical transcriptionist in the 21st century—proficiency with computer operating systems and word processing programs, a greatly expanded medical vocabulary, the ability to use e-mail and the Internet—require much more training than I had had in 1985. Medical transcription has grown in sophistication and acceptance in the last decade. People like myself may be the last of the "accidental" transcriptionists.

In recent years, changes in health care delivery and advances in technology have increased opportunities for medical transcriptionists. A growing and aging population, greater longevity, and the expansion of medical and allied health services have created heightened demand for medical transcriptionists. In addition, cheaper, more powerful home computers have enabled many transcriptionists to work independently, out of their homes.

With this greater opportunity have come new demands, however. Medical transcription requires an ever-increasing level of sophistication as new terms, medications, equipment, and procedures continually appear. Thus a person considering the medical transcription profession should fully understand the personal qualities and training required to succeed. Medical transcriptionists must listen critically to dictated reports from health care providers and analyze that dictation while transcribing it, to screen out possible errors. This process can be as casual as disregarding irrelevant background noise or as complex as questioning an unusual medication dosage or an inconsistency between different parts of a report. The professional medical transcriptionist must combine typing speed and computer skills with an extensive knowledge of medical terminology, anatomy and physiology, pharmacology, medical equipment, and surgical procedures.

For a potential transcriptionist, a strong background in English, an above-average vocabulary, and excellent proofreading skills are all crucial. Facility with word processing and computers is also required. A transcriptionist must also be able to tolerate extended periods of sitting and concentrating. Reduced on-the-job socializing—due to headphone use—may take some adjustment.

For all the emphasis on knowledge, terminology, and understanding, medical transcription remains a production-oriented business. Transcriptionists in an office setting should expect to have to meet high production quotas and accuracy standards. Independent transcriptionists should expect their income to be tied directly to the quantity and quality of their output.

MEDICAL TRANSCRIPTION TRAINING DECISION

Cynthia Lewis

There are a number of options available to those seeking medical transcription training. These include taking local community college or trade school classes, enrolling in distance learning classes, training side by side with another transcriptionist, and, possibly, learning it on your own.

When you research learning opportunities, just be sure any course you sign up for covers *all* of the following: medical terminology; acronyms, eponyms, and abbreviations; anatomy; physiology; laboratory tests and values; medical procedures and equipment; drugs; transcription formatting; ethics of medical transcription; research methods and resources; typing and grammar (if needed); and marketing and other transcription-related business skills. Also check on instructor availability and be sure the course offers *lots* of practice with actual transcription. Ask about the details of each course, find the one that gives you what you want, and then investigate it thoroughly.

A reputable training program will expect you to want to check with its graduates for references. Take the time to talk with former students, and be specific in your inquiries. Ask if the course material prepared them to work in "the real world." Ask how strong the research training was. Get a feel for how extensive the actual transcription practice is and how thorough the anatomy training. You need time to build up your transcription speed to the point where you can make the money you expect to make. When you are paid pennies per line, you must type a lot of lines to make the good income you hope for!

TRAINING FOR TRANSCRIPTIONISTS

Training for a medical transcription career may take several paths, including formal training at community or vocational colleges, home study correspondence courses, and on-line courses available on the World Wide Web. Whatever the format, all courses should provide the transcription student with certain basics:

- A thorough grounding in medical terminology (including Greek and Latin roots), anatomy and physiology, and basic pharmacology
- Graduated experience transcribing actual medical dictations

Training may take from several months to two years, depending on the number of hours per week and the relative comprehensiveness of the program. Busy transcription departments have little time for extended training; therefore, thorough preparation may considerably enhance one's employability.

A vocational aptitude test may be helpful in assessing one's personal suitability for this profession. There are many different types of aptitude tests. They can measure or evaluate such things as a person's analytical reasoning, associative or auditory memory, clerical skills, inductive reasoning, and word association. Strength in areas associated with medical transcription, such as clerical skills and memory, may indicate a natural aptitude for the profession and a higher probability of achieving success on the job. Tests that measure vocational aptitude include the Ball Aptitude Battery™.

You can also evaluate your psychological suitability for a career as a medical transcriptionist, using such tests as the Myers Briggs Type Indicator. This test measures people's tendencies or preferences in four broad areas of personality—extroversion versus introversion, sensing versus intuitive, thinking versus feeling, and judging versus perceiving—yielding a total of 16 different possible types. Understanding your type can help you determine whether a career in medical transcription is appropriate for you. For example, persons with strong tendencies toward extroversion might find the necessary quiet and introspective focus of a medical transcription office uncomfortable.

It also makes sense to analyze the local and regional job market before beginning a training program. This can take the form of clipping and organizing advertisements for local transcription positions, contacting the local chapter of the American Association for Medical Transcription (AAMT), and using local libraries to find employment statistics for the profession in your area. Individuals in smaller communities may find fewer opportunities and less turnover than do those in larger cities. Studying your locale may influence such decisions as whether or not to relocate, how long a training course to enroll in, and what amount of financial support to pursue. Similarly, comparing the salaries and costs of living in different areas may help your decision making and career planning.

Once you have completed your training, you can search for employment across a wide spectrum of specialties and interests within the health care arena. Variety and the opportunity for continual learning are two great advantages of the medical transcription profession. For example, a multispecialty transcriptionist at a major medical center may transcribe, in a single work day, medical, surgical, psychiatric, and varied allied health reports.

The increasing diversity of therapies provided to patients, as well as the expanding sophistication of medical procedures, almost guarantees that new medical terms will continue to appear frequently. Those who make the grade, completing formal training courses and successfully securing employment as a transcriptionist, should have interesting and challenging careers to look forward to. Becoming a medical transcriptionist is a difficult yet financially and personally rewarding goal. Serving as a member of the health care community makes a valuable contribution to society.

HOW TO FIND A GOOD MEDICAL TRANSCRIPTION TRAINING PROGRAM

Penny Nicholls Mann

Medical transcription has become a popular field lately, and transcription schools are popping up all over. Unfortunately, not all of these schools are good programs. I hire transcriptionists for a service in the Atlanta area. If there is one thing I find consistently about recent graduates, it is that they have unrealistic expectations. Many "newbies" expect to work at home and make $30,000 a year as soon as they graduate, when in reality they do not yet have the skills required for such an outcome. I blame this on the inadequate training some have received.

Check with local hospitals, clinics, and transcription services and ask them if they can recommend a training program. Most services test all applicants, and they may have noticed whose graduates pass their tests and whose do not. Since any program's graduates may have different skill levels, employers may not recommend one specific program, but they may give clues about which to avoid—which is sometimes more valuable information.

Ask detailed questions about the curriculum. A course in medical terminology is not enough; you also need exposure to anatomy and physiology, disease pathology, pharmacology, and so on. You will also want access to standard reference books. AAMT style guidelines would be a plus. Transcription practice is the key to medical transcription training.

The following questions should help you determine if the program you are considering makes the grade:

1. How many practice reports are there? An acceptable answer is over one hundred—anything less is an entry-level course that will not prepare you for your first job.
2. What types and formats of reports are covered? The "big four" types of general medical records reports are the history and physical report, the consultation report, the procedure/operative note report, and the discharge summary. SOAP (subjective, objective, assessment, plan) notes are often used for clinics and doctors' offices. ER reports, delivery notes, and other specialty-related reports are usually variations of these types. The broader your knowledge base, the broader your base of potential employers.

HOW TO FIND A GOOD MEDICAL TRANSCRIPTION TRAINING PROGRAM (continued)

3. What is the source of the course's practice dictations? Actual physician dictations from a variety of doctors and settings are the best. The difficulty level should increase as the course goes along. There should be background noise, poor-quality recordings, accents, and rambling dictators.
4. How large are the classes, and how many instructors are there? Some schools have one instructor with a small class, whereas others may use two instructors in a larger class. You want to keep the student-to-teacher ratio as small as possible.
5. Did the instructor transcribe for a living, and if so for how long? Make sure your instructor is, or at least was, an MT with a minimum of three years of experience.
6. What kind of placement services are offered after graduation? Finding that first MT job can be challenging. Make sure the program is going to do something to help you get started. Look for a placement rate of more than 90 percent.

Above all, trust your instincts. You are about to make a career change; the school you choose will become part of your support during this process, and it can make all the difference. You don't want to graduate and find that your training did not prepare you for your new career. Make sure the program you select is the real thing and not "fool's gold."

ORGANIZATIONS FOR TRANSCRIPTIONISTS

AAMT was founded in Modesto, California, by a group of "medical transcribers," including Vera Pyle, Linda Campbell, Sally Pittman, Donna Avila-Weil, and others. Their local organization, the Central Valley Medical Transcribers Association, which they began in 1975, evolved into the national group in 1978. In the 22 years since then AAMT has grown to encompass thousands of members nationally. Its certification program for medical transcriptionists and its publications, including the *Journal of the American Association for Medical Transcription* (JAAMT), the *AAMT Book of Style for Medical Transcription,* the "Medical Transcriptionist's Bill of Rights," and *The Surgical Word Book,* by Claudia Tessier, have set industry standards.

The Health Professions Institute (HPI) publishes the journal *Perspectives,* the SUM (*s*ystems *u*nit *m*ethod) series of medical transcription training tapes, and transcription-related reference books, including *Current Medical Terminology* by Vera Pyle. HPI was founded by Sally Pittman and was previously known as Prima Vera Publications. Its current Web address is http://www.hpisum.com. Both AAMT and HPI contribute valuable information and services to students and professional medical transcriptionists.

Having two such outstanding support organizations benefits the entire profession and helps ensure its continued growth and success. Additionally, a third organization, the Medical Transcription Industry Alliance (MTIA), provides education and information on managing a transcription business, ethical issues, and quality control.

REVIEW QUESTIONS

1. How has the medical transcription profession changed in recent years?
2. What types of training to become a medical transcriptionist are available?
3. What job-related personality characteristics can be identified by the Myers Briggs Type Indicator?
4. How might you evaluate the job market for transcriptionists in your area?

RELATED WEB SITES

Note: All World Wide Web addresses were checked prior to publication, but URLs and links may be subject to change with time.

AMERICAN ASSOCIATION FOR MEDICAL TRANSCRIPTION: http://www.aamt.org/aamt/

ANDREWS SCHOOL OF MEDICAL TRANSCRIPTION: http://www.andrewsschool.com

CALIFORNIA COLLEGE OF HEALTH SCIENCES: http://www.cchs.edu/

CAREER STEP TRAINING CENTER: http://www.careerstep.com

HEALTH PROFESSIONS INSTITUTE: http://www.hpisum.com

MEDICAL TRANSCRIPTION EDUCATION CENTER, INC.: http://www.mtecinc.com

MEDICAL TRANSCRIPTION INDUSTRY ALLIANCE: http://www.mtia.com

MEDITECH DISTANCE LEARNING PROGRAM: http://www.meditec.com

NEW MEDICAL TRANSCRIPTIONISTS CONNECTION: http://www.mtexchange.com

REVIEW OF SYSTEMS SCHOOL OF MEDICAL TRANSCRIPTION: http://www.mtmonthly.com/ros/index.html

2
Beginning the Job Search

LEARNING OBJECTIVES

- Discuss preparations for your job search that you should begin while still in school
- List five important elements of a professional transcription position
- Develop a personal ranking of job elements, in order of their importance to you
- List five different types of medical transcription workplaces

ON-THE-JOB PROFILE
The One-Day Job Offer

While employed by a temporary service some years ago, I was told to report to an office on the far north side of town at 8:00 A.M. Not having a car at that time, I consulted the bus schedule. I found that if I took a 6:30 bus, changed to another, and walked about 10 blocks I could be there on time. That's exactly what I did.

I arrived at 7:50 and knocked on the front door. The manager opened the door with a puzzled look on his face.

"Who are you?" he asked.

"I'm from the temporary service. They told me 8 o'clock."

"But," the manager said, surprised, "you're *early.*"

"I took the early bus. Where do I sit?"

"We've never had anyone early up here," said the manager, escorting me inside. He showed me to my desk, and I was indeed the first one there. His regular employees weren't even in yet. I started looking over the work, and once the regulars came in someone showed me the steps involved in word processing the forms they used.

It took me a while to get a rhythm going. However, by that afternoon I was rolling along, making good speed, concentrating on my work. I had the impression that my coworkers were very familiar with the program but were not particularly fast or enthusiastic typists. So I was a bit surprised when the manager called

---

ON-THE-JOB PROFILE   (continued)

me into his office at 4:00 P.M., as I felt I'd done my best under new and challenging circumstances.

"I'd like to offer you a permanent position," he said. "You type faster than anyone on my staff. You don't fool around. And you show up on time—even early!"

I thanked him warmly for the unexpected job offer.

"I take my work seriously," I told him, "but without a car, I couldn't really get here easily. It took me almost two hours to get here on the bus."

I was sorry to decline his gracious offer, but I shouldn't have been so surprised by it. Employers need reliable, responsible people who don't waste time making personal calls or daydreaming when they're being paid to work. Whatever the job may be, if it's important enough to pay someone to do it, it must be important enough for the employee to do it well!

Managers notice.

Doing what you're assigned to do, when you're assigned to do it, will rarely work against you. Showing up early instead of 10 minutes late is a sign of respect, and there can never be too much respect in any job.

Your search for a professional medical transcription position should begin before you complete your training. Preparing for and researching a successful job hunt goes hand in hand with learning to transcribe. Research done during training will provide a solid starting point for when your coursework is completed.

I recommend keeping a job scrapbook as a basic method of researching local employers. Each week during your training, clip, date, and file local employment advertisements for medical transcriptionists. The purpose in doing this is not to build a list of *jobs,* since most of the jobs you see advertised will be filled by the time you finish your training, but rather to build a list of *employers* who hire medical transcriptionists. A well-kept scrapbook, compiled over several months, may indicate which employers regularly advertise for transcriptionists, what shifts may be available, what the necessary qualifications are, and who various contact persons are. Employers who state in their ads that they hire new graduates should be highlighted, with their ads filed separately in the front of the scrapbook.

Researching your job hunt may also take the form of joining the local chapter of AAMT (based in Modesto, California) to begin developing a network of transcription contacts. Student memberships are available. The many benefits of AAMT membership are listed on their Web site (http://www.aamt.org/aamt). These include a subscription to the *Journal of the American Association for Medical Transcription* (JAAMT), the ability to participate in over 130 local AAMT chapters and state and regional associations, access to medical reference publications, and extensive continuing education opportunities. Attending local meetings can provide an opportunity to meet working transcriptionists and transcription employers. Also, membership in AAMT demonstrates a professional attitude.

Another avenue of research to pursue while still in school is to contact the nearest medical or public library. Ask for information related to medical transcription, local directories of medical facilities and physicians, and information on medical job lines (telephone numbers with recorded information on current job openings). Check job lines each week and write down any information related to transcription positions.

During the final months of your coursework, planning for your job hunt should become more concrete. Having researched a good base of possible employers to draw from will help you narrow your focus and conduct a successful job search.

JOB HUNT PLANNING LIST

The following paragraphs discuss ten important elements to consider when hunting for a transcription job.

Job Location

Plan to limit your job hunt to areas that are within a reasonable commute from your home (one hour or less each way), unless you are willing to relocate. Job opportunities outside this radius should be assigned lower priority, unless local jobs are scarce or a particularly attractive position warrants an extended commute. If you will have to rely on public transportation to get to work, ride and time the appropriate bus or subway routes in advance.

Record travel time to employment interviews and factor in likely rush hour delays. Add preparation time, travel time, and employment hours for a clear picture of the entire work-day. Keep in mind that a one-hour daily commute (30 minutes each way) adds up to 250 hours of commuting per year. Also, the farther away the job, the higher the transportation expenses, reducing your net income. The relative convenience of driving versus the aggravation of dealing with traffic should also be considered.

Working Hours

Both full-time and part-time work are available in medical transcription. Needs vary among different employers and over time for individual employers (because of seasonal workload fluctuations, sudden staff changes, the acquisition of new contracts, and so on). Flexibility, whenever possible, is helpful in finding employment opportunities, especially for new graduates. This is particularly true for hospitals and other 24-hour facilities, where evening, nighttime, or weekend shifts may be difficult to staff. New hires willing to work less popular shifts, either regularly or in rotation with existing staff, may be more readily placed. At the same time, care should be taken to obtain a reasonably acceptable schedule from the start; do not assume your employer will improve your schedule later on. On-call work is another option, although it is a less reliable source of income.

Working Conditions

Medical transcription is a production-based business that requires sitting and typing for extended periods of time. Transcription offices can range from pleasant, spacious environments to windowless "boiler rooms."

Working conditions are an important component of overall job satisfaction—perhaps as important as salary. A positive work space has adequate light and large windows, reasonable air quality, ergonomic chairs and workstations, adequate space between desks, a relatively quiet environment, and modern computers with full-color monitors. Remember, though, that new hires have less leverage than experienced transcriptionists and may need to accept less-than-optimal conditions at first.

Wages

New transcriptionists may find several payment options available. First is the standard hourly wage, with benefits. This wage can vary widely between states, and even within cities, in the broad $8- to $20-per-hour range. Some employers also offer "incentive pay" for outstanding production or exceptional quality.

Transcriptionists may also be paid on a per-line basis, and some work as independent contractors, supplying their own benefits. New transcriptionists may fare better with a reliable hourly wage.

What constitutes a "living wage" for any given individual depends on the cost of living in his or her area as well as the individual's family situation and overall financial picture. Figuring the net, or "take home," pay will help you judge the adequacy of a "gross" wage offer. Matching income to expected expenses—allowing for unexpected difficulties—will help as you weigh salary offers. Initial positions may not meet your expectations but will provide the necessary experience for subsequent raises.

Benefits

Most regular transcription positions include benefits. Good benefits add significantly to the value of any salary. Paid vacation, sick leave, medical and dental insurance, pension plans, and short- and long-term disability insurance are benefits that may—or may not—be included in a job offer. Clarifying benefits during the interviewing process will help you compare job offers. If you are considering part-time work, ask how many hours per week are required to obtain full (or partial) benefits. Additionally, inquire if benefits begin at the time of hire or if there is a substantial waiting period (sometimes up to 90 days) before they take effect. Unfortunately, the current trend in nearly every industry is toward reducing employee benefits, so you should anticipate receiving offers with reduced benefits.

Job-Related Expenses

Job-related expenses include the cost of professional attire, which in the case of medical transcriptionists can vary from very casual to standard business dress; costs for food, which can vary considerably depending on whether or not a subsidized cafeteria or lunchroom is available; union dues, which may be mandatory or optional; parking fees, if not paid for by the employer; costs for daycare, if necessary; and the price of reference books, if they are not supplied by the employer.

Coworkers

Information about the workers at a given medical office or transcription service can reveal much about the office environment. For example, average number of years of transcription experience indicates a department's depth and maturity. Experienced transcriptionists can offer guidance and reference assistance, saving newcomers valuable time and expanding their knowledge base. Once hired, a new employee should match the names and faces of co-workers as soon as possible.

Production Standards

As wages vary, so do production requirements. Production is often judged in terms of lines or minutes of dictation transcribed per hour. Since the switch from typewriters to word processors in the late 1980s, production requirements have increased. Pressures for cost control, ever-greater efficiency, and high individual output will likely continue. Realistic standards of 100 to 150 lines per hour (based on a 6.5 inch line length) can be met by a diligent, skilled transcriptionist. Standards of 150 and above may require advanced word expansion software. Some employers set lower production targets for new hires in their first months of employment; this should be discussed in the interview.

Quality Standards

Transcriptionists strive for 100 percent accuracy but must balance that goal against production quotas, human nature, and the variable quality and intelligibility of medical dictation. Output above 98 percent accuracy, although possible, may not always be attainable in the real world. Medical transcriptionists working eight-hour or longer shifts are subject to the same fatigue and reduced efficiency of other production workers. Therefore, the transcribing process must include adequate time for proofreading and spell checking. It is a good idea to ask about a prospective employer's quality standards during the interview.

Opportunities for Advancement

Although a medical transcription position may seem like "an end in itself," preparing for eventual advancement is always a consideration. Advanced positions include lead transcriptionist, transcription editor and proofreader, transcription supervisor, transcription instructor, and transcription service manager. Also, continuing education opportunities provided by employers may promote long-term career development. In the near future, the World Wide Web may also provide opportunities for independent medical transcriptionists to incorporate medical research and on-line searching into their professional services.

IS THIS CAREER FOR YOU?

Cynthia Lewis

Medical transcription is the process of producing reports from dictation by medical providers of the details of patient office visits; clinical, radiological, and operative procedures; and so on. In addition to typing the reports into the desired formats, transcriptionists also verify the accuracy of the dictation. To do this, a transcriptionist must have a solid foundation in English grammar, medical terminology, anatomy and physiology, and pharmacology, and an understanding of laboratory tests and values and medical equipment and procedures. Just having a computer at home and knowing how to type is definitely not enough to become a working, successful medical transcriptionist. If you don't love the English language, if you have to check the dictionary as you sign your name, if hyphens and apostrophes give you cold chills, then forget medical transcription—it's not for you.

There are many different working environments available to a trained, experienced medical transcriptionist, including hospitals; clinics; individual and group medical, chiropractic, radiology practices; and local and national transcription services.

Although medical transcription appears to be an excellent field for people who would like to move from another career to working at home, those intending to make this move need to be aware of a potential "Catch-22" in doing so: because of the difficulty of the work, it is sometimes difficult for "newbies" to get a job or clients without experience. I feel that if you are committed to this career, take a reputable MT training course, really learn all that the course covers, have outstanding English language skills, own a comprehensive library of references, and possess excellent research skills, then you can do it.

TYPES OF TRANSCRIPTION FACILITIES

A key decision to be made in planning your job hunt is the type of setting you would like to work in. Many different types of facilities require medical transcriptionists, and they often have quite different characteristics. Facilities that may use medical transcriptionists include physicians' offices, clinics, intermediate care facilities, hospitals, major medical centers/teaching hospitals, psychiatric facilities, radiology and pathology labs, allied health services, and transcription services. Self-employment is another option. A description of each type of setting follows.

Physicians' Offices

Working in this setting includes transcribing reports for one or more physicians, possibly in family practice or internal medicine, and may include transcribing some acute care reports. In smaller offices, medical transcriptionists may be asked to perform other duties, such as answering phones or maintaining medical records. For the new transcriptionist, the lower level of difficulty and smaller number of dictators to learn may provide a smooth entry into the profession. Disadvantages could include an excess of nontranscription duties, lower-than-expected salary, and lack of intellectual challenge.

Clinics

Clinics may combine family practice and internal medicine with specialties such as otorhinolaryngology, ophthalmology, and orthopedics. Larger clinics provide new transcriptionists with a good introduction to multispecialty work, but at a less intense level than in hospitals. Allied health providers such as physician's assistants, nurse practitioners, and various therapists may also dictate.

Intermediate Care Facilities

Changes in health care delivery that have reduced hospital patient loads have also expanded roles for intermediate care facilities, which provide care for patients not yet ready for independent living after a hospital stay. These facilities may combine long-term beds, such as in nursing homes, with minor "walk-in" emergency rooms, operating rooms, and even intensive care units.

Hospitals

Hospitals usually require two years of multispecialty transcription experience. This requirement may be negotiable for skilled newer transcriptionists willing to work evening, nighttime, or weekend shifts. However, the level of difficulty of hospital dictation should not be underestimated. Reports transcribed may include hospital admission and discharge reports, transfer summaries, procedure and operative reports, consultations, and even psychiatric and therapeutic reports. A high level of knowledge and performance is expected from the hospital transcriptionist. Advantages include interesting and varied work and frequent learning opportunities. Job stress, related to high production standards and "stat," or "right away," dictations is a potential disadvantage.

Major Medical Centers/Teaching Hospitals

Teaching hospitals, or hospitals at major university medical centers, provide the transcriptionist with a regular supply of new dictators as resident physicians rotate through their training. Advanced medical students may also provide dictation. Major medical centers may also perform experimental procedures, test new drug protocols, and provide cutting-edge treatment in such fields as oncology and interventional radiology.

Psychiatric Facilities

Dedicated psychiatric facilities sometimes use transcriptionists, and hospital work sometimes includes psychiatric reports as well. The formats and terms used for psychiatric reports differ from those used for medical reports. Psychiatric evaluations may be independent, or they may be incorporated into medical "screening evaluations." Advantages of working on psychiatric reports include learning more about the inner workings of the human mind and human behavior.

Radiology and Pathology Labs

Radiology and pathology are two medical specialties that require extensive medical transcription. A new transcriptionist may find it easier to begin with a single discipline and gradually develop multispecialty skills. Although some radiological reports, such as those for chest x-rays, may be quite routine and conform largely to preset "macros," more complex procedures will challenge and inform. Pathology transcription can develop knowledge of anatomy and laboratory values.

Allied Health Services

In recent years, increased referrals to many types of therapists have expanded patient care. A physician or other health care provider may refer a patient to a physical, vocational, speech, or occupational therapist, as needed. This evolving diversification of care provides new opportunities for the medical transcriptionist. Allied health reports may be included in extended medical reports, or they may be entirely separate.

Transcription Services

Transcription services are independent businesses that contract with health care facilities to provide transcription services. There are both local and national services. Transcriptionists working for a transcription service may be paid on a production or an hourly basis and may or may not receive benefits. The terms of employment should be clearly understood, particularly regarding one's status as either an employee of the service or an independent contractor. Services that hire on a contract basis might not deduct income or Social Security taxes, and in such cases it is the transcriptionist's responsibility to make quarterly tax payments to the federal government and—unless your state does not collect income tax—the appropriate state government. A national directory of transcription services is available—*The Nationwide Medical Transcription Service Directory* from MediScript Transcription, P.O. Box 705, Roanoke, IN 46783.

Self-Employment

The new medical transcriptionist, with a modern home computer and transcriber, also has the option of being self-employed. However, the choice to work at home independently requires careful consideration. Just as hospitals generally require two years of experience, the challenges of independent transcribing will be better handled after one to two years of experience in an office setting.

Additionally, running one's own business requires entrepreneurial skills that take time to develop. Persons considering self-employment may want to begin by working at home as telecommuters or by working half-time as employees and half-time independently to start.

REVIEW QUESTIONS

1. What are three important characteristics of a positive work space?
2. Are transcription wages generally lower or higher in rural areas than they are in urban areas?
3. How would transcribing for a clinic differ from transcribing for a major hospital?
4. What information can a job hunt scrapbook provide?
5. What would be a reasonable production standard, in terms of lines per hour?
6. What would be a reasonable quality standard, in terms of percentage of accuracy?

RELATED WEB SITES

AMERICA ONLINE (keyword *Medical Transcription*)
MTDAILY: http://www.mtdaily.com
THE MEDICAL TRANSCRIPTIONIST'S JOBS DIGEST: http://www.intlhomeworkers.com/MT/
INTERNET RESOURCES FOR MEDICAL TRANSCRIPTIONISTS: http://www.mtuniverse.com
HEALTH CARE AND MEDICAL EMPLOYMENT: http://www.pohly.com/links.shtml

3
The Job Search Process

LEARNING OBJECTIVES

- Suggest several resources for locating transcription job openings
- Describe several possible tests that could be given to a transcription applicant
- Describe good preparation for a personal job interview
- Explain the rationale behind sending follow-up letters to potential employers

 ON-THE-JOB PROFILE

Trial Offers

When I was teaching transcription, several of my students came to me with unusual dilemmas related to unexpected job offers. It's one thing to go out and "beat the bushes" to find a job, but quite another to have one fall into your lap before you are ready!

The first, I recall, was a fine student who had just graduated. Although she lacked professional experience, she applied with a transcription service in her home town of Everett, Washington. She did very well on her transcription test, and they were impressed but not entirely convinced. They asked her to work for a one-month trial period at $5 per hour; if she was successful, they would then hire her at their regular professional rate.

I knew that, like most students, her finances were tight, and a month of low wages would be a hardship. However, I urged her to take the job if she possibly could.

"Look at the long-term benefit," I suggested. "If you can stick it out for four weeks, you're in! Over the course of a year, you haven't lost much money, and you have a professional position with a chance to switch to production pay. I'd jump on it!"

She accepted my advice, despite her misgivings, and took the trial offer. Upon its completion she was offered a permanent position at full pay. In a few months, the "hardship" of the trial was forgotten.

ON-THE-JOB PROFILE   (continued)

Another student had an even more surprising experience. She was only halfway through the one-year evening transcription course and was also working full-time during the day as a secretary in an oncology office. A physician from another practice phoned her office and incidentally mentioned that his transcriptionist had just quit. Did she know of anyone she might recommend?

"What can I do?" she asked me that night. "I'm only halfway through the course!"

"You call him back tomorrow," I said sternly, "and say you're only halfway through a one-year training course, but would he like a 60-day trial to see if you can meet his needs? Plus, you agree to finish the course so he has a fully trained transcriptionist."

She took my rather firm suggestion, and the doctor took her up on her offer of a 60-day trial period. At the end of those 60 days, the job was permanently hers. She had done such excellent work in class, I had no doubts of her ability on the job.

A third example concerned at-home employment, which usually requires at least one to two years of office experience. I was contacted by a busy transcription manager on Seattle's Eastside who needed not one but two transcriptionists, right away, to work out of their homes. I had several students who were just preparing to graduate, and two quickly came to mind: Jamie and Michelle. Jamie's work had been unfailingly accurate throughout the course. Michelle had been a tremendous researcher, poring over the medical reference books in class and eager to learn, learn, learn! I told the employer about them and that they were new grads of the highest quality.

Both were hired.

A month later I spoke with Michelle and asked her how things were going.

"I got stuck all the time the first few weeks," she said, "and had to call the boss a lot. But things are getting better—and I'm at home with my child!"

Jamie, too, had had difficulties, but she stuck with it. Their trial had been the work itself, and persevering had earned them their positions. Their supervisor knew they were worth developing, and my faith in them had been completely justified.

Although there are many techniques and strategies for job hunting, their effectiveness can vary with individual differences, geographical regions, and local economic conditions. However, it is always valuable to know basic techniques for finding job openings, applying for a job, interviewing, and following up. Once you have mastered the basics, you can select from a variety of strategies for the best approach to use for your own individual search.

FINDING JOB OPENINGS

Locating medical transcription job openings involves developing a logical and realistic search method. This method can include looking for publicly advertised positions; researching in-house positions advertised only internally, within a hospital or medical office; contacting prospective employers that are not currently advertising; studying local medical newsletters and directories of local medical employers; letting friends, relatives, and other personal contacts in the health professions know that you are looking; and scanning Internet postings and research.

Looking for Publicly Advertised Positions

Although most employers that advertise openings in newspapers place their ads in the Sunday classifieds, daily inspection of classified ads is recommended. Obtaining a newspaper in the morning before business hours provides the opportunity to move quickly on desirable positions. Look for ads under "medical transcription" and "transcription," scan subheadings in larger hospital and clinic display ads, and consider other possible listings, such as under "clerical" or "secretarial services." File all transcription ads for reference and to build an employer data-base. Follow advertisement directions closely in regard to the employer's preferred method of contact, such as by phone, in person, or by fax.

Researching In-House Positions

Health care facilities often have employment bulletin boards posted for employee convenience. The positions posted there may not necessarily be externally advertised. Regular visits to nearby health care facilities may provide valuable information on internal job openings. You can also contact the human resources offices of health care facilities. If no medical transcription positions are posted, request an appointment to visit the transcription department, and express a keen interest in working there.

Contacting Prospective Employers Not Presently Advertising

A personal visit to a potential employer will always have more impact than simply mailing a resume. This shows the employer your strong interest in applying for a position with the organization. However, as transcription offices are often busy, it is a good idea to call first and ask permission to stop by. If no positions are currently available, ask if you can check back the following month. Keep a log of contact persons, locations visited, dates, and phone numbers for follow-ups.

Studying Local Medical Newsletters and Directories

Local medical publications, published either by local AAMT chapters or by local hospitals or medical associations, may contain employment opportunities. Local medical directories may also list smaller health care facilities not mentioned elsewhere. In addition, national journals such as the *Journal of the American Association for Medical Transcription* sometimes include transcription positions in various cities.

Using Word of Mouth

Personal contact with friends, relatives, and health care professionals to let them know you are looking expands the number of people involved in your job search. A two-step inquiry is advised, such as, "Do you know of any positions; if not, do you know anyone who may?"

Scanning the Internet

On-line services such as America Online have regional and major city sections that sometimes include job information. Also, there are extensive job listings on the Internet, as well as opportunities to post "electronic" resumes. Some sites of interest are http://www.careermosaic.com and http://www.monster.com.

APPLYING FOR JOBS

After you have identified job openings or potential openings, you can begin the application process. This process has several preliminary steps, including preparing a resume, selecting appropriate professional attire and grooming oneself appropriately, and obtaining and completing a job application.

A resume is a tool for selling yourself to a prospective employer. It provides the employer with information on your background and training. It should communicate, on one page, your name, address, and phone; your education; your relevant work experience; your computer skills; your professional affiliations; and your personal distinctions. The most recent education and work experience should be placed first. A resume should be printed on a home computer or professionally, on high-quality paper. Your resume can be turned in with your completed job application.

Professional attire and good grooming are essential for making a good first impression. Cleanliness, neatness, and businesslike clothing (a dress or pants suit for women, a coat and tie for men) will show a potential employer that you have a professional approach—even if you are only visiting the human resources office for an application.

When requesting a job application, take the opportunity to introduce yourself, describe your qualifications, and state your reason for applying. Consider typing the application (some copy shops still rent typewriters) rather than hand writing it, for a more professional look. Fill out the application as completely and accurately as possible, paying special attention to providing phone numbers of previous employers to allow reference checks. If personal references are requested, ask their permission in advance. Care in preparing a job application suggests that similar care will be taken in the desired transcription position.

MY STORY

Susan K. Hamlin

My interest in becoming a medical transcriptionist began after I had been work-ing for my county government for 15 years. I had a back problem, which I was supposed to be treating with frequent rest and heat applications. No way to do that in an office! I decided on medical transcription because I've always been a good typist and I enjoy working with words.

I started a home-based course, using an electric typewriter for the lessons since I did not have a computer. Later I took a refund of my retirement money, bought a computer, and taught myself PC skills. As soon as I finished the course, with a 96 percent, I mailed out flyers with resumes to all the physicians, hospitals, and clinics in the area. This is a fairly small area, and when that attempt failed, I contacted the other transcriptionists I could find in the phone book. They didn't want to take me on, either.

By that time I was on the Internet. The MT Daily site had the e-mail ad-dresses of a number of medical transcriptionists. I sent an e-mail to every tran-scriptionist listed in California. Someone finally forwarded my letter and resume to someone they knew who took on new transcriptionists, and thus I am now working. The service is based in Rochester, New York, with an office in Califor-nia. I re-record from an outgoing dictation and send the work back by e-mail at-tachment. They started me at six cents a line; I'm now at seven. It was hard at first but is getting easier. The account they have me on now is mostly discharge sum-maries and operative notes. I feel that once I have more experience in this current job, I will have the background to either start my own business or obtain more subcontract work through others.

TAKING EMPLOYMENT TESTS

A prospective employer may require you to take one or more tests in addition to sub-mitting to a personal interview. These may cover, among other things, spelling, editing, proofreading, medical definitions, medical abbreviations, and actual transcription of dictation. The following paragraphs discuss these testing subjects in more detail, and the accompanying boxes include examples of the types of questions a candidate might encounter on a qualifying test for a position as a medical transcriptionist.

Spelling

Spelling tests can include both general and medical terms. Frequently misspelled gen-eral words (such as *accommodate*) are favored, as are commonly mistaken medical terms (such as *tinnitus* and *funduscopic*). Often test takers are asked to circle the correctly (or incorrectly) spelled words. *Paying close attention to test instructions is essential.*

SAMPLE APPLICANT TEST 1

Medical Spelling

CIRCLE THE *INCORRECT* WORDS:

1. Pruritis
2. Humerus
3. Navicular
4. Thryoid
5. Larynx
6. Pharnyx
7. Costochondritis
8. Uvula
9. Metatarsil
10. Scalpel
11. Catheter
12. Cannula
13. Rhynoplasty
14. Neumonia
15. Carcinogen
16. Plazma
17. Stethoscope
18. Medial

Editing

Editing tests may involve correcting grammar and spelling, including ensuring consistent verb tense; capitalization; continuity; or making sure a transcribed report "makes sense."

SAMPLE APPLICANT TEST 2

Grammar

CIRCLE THE *INCORRECT* SENTENCES:

1. We were going to the hospital to visit our cousin after his illness.
2. You said we was never to go there again.
3. As a matter of fact, we don't never attend family functions.
4. There is no reason to avoid a routine physical examination.
5. The best defense against becoming ill are an ounce of prevention.
6. Have you spoke with the nurse about your cousin?
7. Nevertheless, the patient left the hospital against medical advice.
8. We were thoroughly pleased with the care given by the nurses.
9. The hospital food were surprisingly tasty on our last visit.
10. Let's keep the correct use of the objective case just between you and I.

Proofreading

Proofreading tests may include comparing side-by-side lists for accuracy, finding errors in transcribed dictation, and checking numbers as well as words (for laboratory test results and medication dosages). *Material to be proofed may not always contain mistakes.*

SAMPLE APPLICANT TEST 3

Proofreading

CIRCLE THE *INCORRECT* WORDS IN THE FOLLOWING PARAGRAPH:

The patient is a 64-year-old man with a hitsory of a fall from a ladder with possible fracture. He was brought to the emergincy room via ambulans for evaluation and treatment. His vital signs included a temprature of 37 Celsius, blood pressure 134/88, puls 72 and a respratory rate of 18. Physical examination noted several lacerations on the hands and fourarms, which were treated. Additionly, an x-ray of the left wrist was taken which was negitive for fraxure. The patient was sent to Telematry for overnight observation, and the family was contacted. The patient's care will be turned over to Dr. Johnson, and the patient care corodinator will be notafied.

Medical Definitions

Some tests ask the applicant to define common medical terms. Tests may also include anatomical terms (such as *fibula* or *clavicle*) to assess the candidate's knowledge of anatomy.

Medical Abbreviations

Knowledge of abbreviations in common use may be tested. Such abbreviations are used to indicate dosage frequency (*b.i.d.* for "twice a day," *p.r.n.* for "as needed"), specific illnesses or difficulties (*MI* for "myocardial infarction," *CVA* for "cerebrovascular accident"), or basic medical shorthand (*WNL* for "within normal limits").

SAMPLE APPLICANT TEST 4

Medical Abbreviations

CIRCLE THE *CORRECT* MEANING:

1. t.i.d.
   A. Triple in diameter
   B. This is done
   C. Three times a day
2. wnl
   A. Will not last
   B. Within normal limits
   C. Weigh no longer
3. p.r.n.
   A. Please return
   B. Per registered nurse
   C. As needed

4. ncat
   A. no change after this
   B. normocephalic, atraumatic
   C. not catching and temporary
5. perrl
   A. pearl-colored skin
   B. post every regulation
   C. pupils equal, round, and reactive
      to light

Transcribing

Whether or not other tests are required, a transcription test is almost certain to be required. Transcription supervisors need a demonstration of applicants' transcription ability to fairly and realistically evaluate job candidates. The ability to listen carefully and accurately and promptly transcribe what has been said will be closely assessed. Excellent performance on a transcription test may help compensate for lack of formal work experience.

INTERVIEWING

In addition to whatever tests may be required, the transcription supervisor might also want a personal interview with the applicant. This interview has several purposes. It allows the supervisor to learn more about the candidate's background and personality than his or her resume provides and to see how the candidate responds under stress. On the positive side, it offers the job applicant the chance to further explain his or her qualifications, demonstrate interest and enthusiasm for the position, and find out more about job benefits and responsibilities.

Preparing for a job interview, like preparing for an important test, includes getting a good night's sleep and eating a moderate breakfast. In addition, a shower and professional attire are both essential. If possible, schedule the interview at a good time, not at lunchtime or too close to 5:00. Late morning, or after the supervisor's lunch hour, may be best. Be sure the time is convenient for the prospective employer. Bring extra copies of your resume, and allow adequate time to arrive early. A brief walk prior to entering the office may be relaxing.

During the interview, use good eye contact, sit up straight, and be sincere. Answer questions honestly, without talking too much. *Allow the interviewer to conduct the interview.* Have questions in mind, either written down or memorized, to ask if an opportunity to do so is offered. Asking polite, thoughtful questions is one way of demonstrating interest in the position.

Expect "ringers"—questions designed to catch a candidate off guard. These may include asking your reason for leaving a previous position, questions about your honesty and integrity ("Have you ever stolen anything from a workplace?"), questions about your interactions with previous coworkers and supervisors ("What did you like *least* about the people you worked with?"), asking how you respond to pressure ("What would you tell an angry doctor who called saying his STAT report didn't print?"), and inquiries about your future plans ("What do you expect to be doing five years from now?").

Because interviewing and taking the accompanying tests is stressful, limit interviews to one or two per day. The goal is not to do a maximal number of interviews but to do as well as possible in each one you do set up.

FOLLOWING UP

After concluding a job interview and returning home, take time within the following 48 hours to write a personal thank-you letter to the transcription supervisor. Briefly express your thanks for the interview and your sincere interest in the position you applied for. Mail this letter promptly. This small act of courtesy may have a significant positive effect on the interviewer, especially if several people apply but only one writes a thank-you note. A personal thanks indicates a thoughtful person who might be pleasant to work with. Harmony and cooperation are essential in running an effective transcription department.

After the interview, allow time for the supervisor to evaluate all of the candidates. If you are not contacted within two weeks, phone for a progress report, unless you were specifically told that the process would take longer. Thereafter, follow up each week until the position is filled or you secure other employment.

REVIEW QUESTIONS

1. How can a prospective medical transcriptionist identify "in-house" positions?
2. What sorts of tests may be required of applicants for transcription jobs in addition to a transcribing test?
3. What is the best preparation for a personal interview?
4. How soon should a follow-up letter of thanks be written after a personal interview?
5. Is speed or accuracy more important in a transcription test?
6. Should an applicant include contact phone numbers of previous employers on a job application?

RELATED WEB SITES

CONDUCTING A JOB SEARCH AND JOB HUNTING TECHNIQUES: http://www.mapping-your-future. org/planning/thejobse.htm

QUINTESSENTIAL CAREER GUIDE AND JOB HUNTING RESOURCES GUIDE: http://www.stetson.edu/ ~rhansen/careers.html

MANAGE YOUR CAREER: http://www.excite.com/careers/career_hub/manage/

4
Job Search Strategies

LEARNING OBJECTIVES

- List five "nonstandard" job search strategies
- Create a sample "trial offer" to present to an employer
- Explain the difference between job creation and job focusing
- List three ways to obtain overflow work
- Discuss the key differences between standard and nonstandard job search strategies

ON-THE-JOB PROFILE
Job Focusing

My wife, a registered nurse, has used job focusing on several occasions to find work exactly where she wanted it. Three years ago she worked far from our Seattle home, on the east side of Lake Washington. Tired of her commute, she grew interested in a small intermediate care facility that was just a 10-minute drive from our house. On a hunch, she contacted them—but rather than apply directly for a nursing position, she offered her skills as a CPR instructor, for free. They wasted no time in accepting her generosity. Over a one-year period, while still working on the Eastside, she conducted free monthly CPR classes for the hospital staff. Through that process she got to know both staff and management.

After a year, their staff development coordinator left for another position. This time my wife applied for the job, and her combination of prior teaching experience and personal contact with the staff did the trick. Suddenly the free service became a 24-hour-a-week, well-paying managerial position.

In her new role she ran hospital orientation, taught the facility's CPR classes, and began developing a significant volunteer program. With volunteer help, she established a small medical library. By the end of the second year, her position was full-time, and the work had expanded to include organizing advanced cardiac life support classes, CPR instructor training classes, and the videotaping of

ON-THE-JOB PROFILE (continued)

physicians' lectures. Afterward, the purchase of the small intermediate care facility by a national hospital chain raised the possibility of her setting up a regional training center for nursing homes.

All this came from her deciding to work at a specific place, focusing on one location, and taking the time to make an opportunity happen. Once such a decision is made, a job seeker may have many options besides "business as usual" to create or obtain a good position.

Finding a job, in any field, is a job in itself. Finding a suitable medical transcription position requires a combination of research, legwork, energy, and strategy. The skills developed in studying medical transcription (attention to detail, perseverance, concentration) must now be applied to the "real world." Once you understand the job search *process*, developing a job search *strategy* will help you pursue that process more efficiently.

To allow for individual differences, you should consider and try out several strategies. Different search strategies may work better for different people and in different regions. Current economic conditions, seasonal fluctuations in employment, and location may all have significant effects on preferable tactics.

This chapter discusses the following topics related to job search strategies: standard job-hunting style, internships, job focusing, job creation, lateral transfers, trial offers, overflow situations, piggybacking, job sharing and combining, business creation, job fairs, temporary employment, screening agencies, the Yellow Pages, word of mouth, and the Internet.

STANDARD JOB-HUNTING STYLE

Most job seekers consult the Sunday paper as their first source of employment opportunities. This may be augmented with calling appropriate job lines, reading trade journals and "alternative" newspapers with job listings, and visiting state employment offices. All of these customary styles of investigation are valid and can produce positive results. Once a job seeker has identified desirable openings, he or she then must decide whether to write, call, or visit prospective employers. Mailing a resume and cover letter is an efficient way to contact multiple employers. The cover letter should indicate the position desired and qualifications related to that position. It should be addressed to the person who has the power to hire. This letter may include a date when a follow-up call will be made.

A direct call to a transcription supervisor is another option. If calling, ask whether it is a convenient time to talk. Once contact is made, an interview is under way—even if you are just requesting an application. Be prepared to answer questions about your previous employment, and have notes and your resume at hand.

A personal visit to request an application is the most effective of the three contact methods. It shows a willingness to expend time and effort in the job search. However, as transcription departments are invariably busy, keep visits brief and to the point. Request an appointment through the human resources office, if possible.

The standard style of job hunting is "slow but steady" and often brings eventual results. It also requires dedication and daily effort, however. Generally speaking, the greater the number of suitable jobs applied for, the higher the chance of success. In addition to this tried-and-true style of job hunting, less traditional strategies deserve mention and investigation by the job applicant. These are discussed in the following paragraphs.

INTERNSHIPS

Some community or technical colleges with medical transcription programs provide internships for their MT students. This is an excellent opportunity for students nearing the end of their coursework to work in an actual transcription office. It gives transcription staff and interns a chance to evaluate and get to know one another in a real work situation. Real-world job experience also supplements the more theoretical classroom activities. If an internship program exists where you are training, take advantage of it. Students without available internships may ask their instructor for permission to contact local employers in that regard.

JOB FOCUSING

Job focusing is a longer-term job-hunting technique that is almost the opposite of the standard trial-and-error method. Job focusing should be used in addition to (not instead of) the standard job search strategy. Rather than seeking numerous jobs and applying until something clicks, in job focusing the prospective applicant researches several likely positions, selects one or two that are most desirable, and *determines* to work there. Even if the desired job is filled by another candidate, the job seeker continues to maintain contact with the preferred employer, on a biweekly or monthly basis. Over a period of time, from weeks to months, the applicant makes regular, courteous inquiries to the employer, expressing a sincere and continued interest in working there. This consistent approach (which may continue until a position is obtained elsewhere) can impress an employer with the applicant's perseverance and interest. Particularly attractive jobs are worth the extra effort; also, supervisors sometimes have the option to open an additional position for an especially dedicated candidate.

JOB CREATION

Surprisingly, jobs can be created as well as applied for. It is completely legitimate to ask health care providers who do not yet dictate reports, or who dictate on a limited basis, if they want to initiate or expand their dictation. Creating a position is an option that changes the job seeker's task to a more active, participatory role. The job seeker might contact not only physicians but also psychologists and allied health care providers (such as physical therapists, occupational therapists, sports medicine practitioners, and so on) and offer transcription services on a part-time, as-needed, or trial basis "to get the ball rolling." (*Note:* If full-time compensation is essential, consider creating two half-time jobs or working full-time at one job and creating a part-time position elsewhere for extra income.)

When creating a new position, pay rates may be quite negotiable. Also, initiating a new position may give the transcriptionist the opportunity to develop standards, policies, and procedures related to transcribing. This experience will carry over into subsequent transcription or even management positions.

ON-THE-JOB PROFILE
Job Creation

In 1982 I was temporarily employed as a cataloger at the Texas State Library. The job was to last for four weeks. During the fourth week, I received an unexpected phone call.

"Hello," said a woman's voice. "This is the Texas Historical Commission. Do you have anyone who can catalog books?"

I indicated that I was a librarian working as a temp. As my job was up Friday at 5:00, I offered to be at the Historical Commission Monday morning at 8:00.

"That will be fine," said the caller.

I arrived Monday morning at 8:00 sharp, expecting a mountain of work to cascade down upon me. Instead, the lady had only 30 books that she wanted cataloged and entered into the existing historical collection—about a week's work.

"I know it's not much," she said, "but you can have an office across the street at the National Register. They are expecting you."

Since I had 30 books to take care of, I accepted the job and lugged the books across the street on a cart. There was, indeed, an empty, rather spacious office for me to work in. I arranged the 30 books on the desk, along with my cataloging tools. I had a week to figure out what to do.

Later that morning, I decided to walk around and introduce myself to the architects and historians who worked at the National Register. There were about a dozen offices in all, plus two secretaries sharing a room. I introduced myself as "the new librarian" and asked each professional if he or she had any books that needed to be cataloged. I struck out the first four or five times. Then, by luck or fate, one of the architects led me over to a small shelf with about 150 books on it.

"These ought to be cataloged," he suggested.

In that very instant, the library for the National Register of Historic Places, Texas division, was founded. As I continued my search, I unearthed another 50 or so books to work on, plus several journal titles scattered here and there. I later discovered that the Texas Historical Commission also had history and archeology collections, both of which needed work.

ON-THE-JOB PROFILE (continued)

I spent the next year building a library from scratch, setting up a card catalog, finding shelves, and requesting funds to order appropriate books to expand the collection. By the second year of operation we had over five hundred titles, and researchers were beginning to drop by, having heard that the National Register had a good architecture library.

In my second year of work, a new editor was hired for the Historical Commission's Texas history publications. He was given the office next to mine. While scanning some arrowhead pictures in an archeology journal one day, I felt him looking over my shoulder.

"That one's called Golondrina," he said, pointing to an arrowhead.

"How do you know?" I asked.

"I discovered it!"

I checked the bibliography, and sure enough, there was his name. We became fast friends, and I was shortly appointed assistant editor, in addition to librarian. From then on I worked on conference publications as well as performing my library duties.

In short, a one-week temporary position had turned into a three-year, once-in-a-lifetime opportunity to build a permanent library of over one thousand volumes. This is a good example of job creation—making a position where none seems to exist, taking the smallest advantage and growing it into a successful job.

LATERAL TRANSFERS

In tight job markets, or if no transcription position is obtained within a reasonable length of time (60–90 days), a lateral transfer within a large organization is a possibility. For example, obtaining a position in medical records at a hospital may give the new transcription graduate a chance to get to know people in the records and transcription departments, and this can facilitate a transfer to transcription later on.

Obviously, a lateral transfer is not the preferred route of entry into medical transcription. However, evening and weekend shifts are often difficult for hospitals to staff and are therefore more readily available. Working off-shifts in a related department will allow the job applicant to continue a daytime search for a transcription position. Making personal contacts in related departments may help the applicant when a transcription position does become available.

ENTRY INTO TRANSCRIPTION

Renee Priest

I sort of stumbled into medical transcription. I had earned a Ph.D. in Russian and fully intended to make a career of translating at the United Nations. When my chil-

ENTRY INTO TRANSCRIPTION (continued)

dren came along, I wanted something I could do from home, so I could be there when they were young. Someone told me of a medical transcription program, and off I went. I have to admit I had not a clue in the world what I was getting myself into.

I graduated from a two-year program and passed both portions of the certified medical transcriptionist exam a year after graduating. I was one of the very, very lucky ones who was able to work from home from day one. I was blessed to find a supervisor who nurtured me, mentored me, and allowed me the freedom to develop my skills at my own pace.

Our service primarily does hospital overflow, currently handling 11 different hospitals. I work on high production and love every second of it.

I work very long hours, six days a week—my personal choice.

I was fortunate enough to stumble on a profession that challenges me, stimulates my mind, and is never boring—one I will be able to do for as long as my brain cells are functioning. When I think about it, I am actually prouder of my CMT designation than I am of my degree in Russian. I had to work really hard to learn this profession, and I still work hard to continue to learn all I must know to do this job properly.

TRIAL OFFERS

Many ads for transcription jobs state that two years of transcription experience is required. Yet, everyone has to start somewhere. Being prepared to agree to a trial period, if necessary, might help compensate for a lack of experience.

For example, transcription employers might request a two- to four-week "free trial" period or request a 30- to 60-day trial period at reduced pay. The actual offer of employment will depend on successful completion of the trial period. Acceptance of this trial is entirely up to the job applicant. However, keep in mind that a one- or even two-month period of low pay is insignificant if it leads to years of well-compensated employment. (Understandably, individual financial circumstances may rule out accepting a period of reduced pay.)

A job applicant might proactively suggest a trial period and leverage that suggestion into an entry-level position. Making this suggestion also demonstrates confidence in the excellence of one's work. Timing this suggestion is crucial—it should not be offered except in a personal interview. Reserve any such offers for the most desirable jobs; even then, suggest a trial period only if necessary to tip the balance in your favor.

OVERFLOW SITUATIONS

Transcription workloads are unpredictable and can vary with seasons, changes in public health, vacation schedules, epidemics, and many other factors. At any given time, transcription departments may be slow, busy, or absolutely swamped! When a crisis occurs and the workload is overwhelming, an opportunity may exist for a new graduate to help out. This can be true in hospital and clinic transcription offices, at transcription services, and also for independent transcriptionists. Extra coverage is always needed for vacations, illnesses, maternity and bereavement leave, as well as unusually heavy workloads. Being available for "on-call" duty may provide a means of entry, and it is possible for a temporary overflow position to continue for some time or even mature into a permanent position.

PIGGYBACKING

"Piggybacking" refers to drawing on the success of other job seekers in your attempts to enter the job market. To make use of this strategy, you need a network of contacts among fellow job hunters. You can develop such a network by getting the phone numbers of fellow transcription students and keeping in touch with them, by attending local meetings of transcription organizations, and so on. Once you are actively job hunting, contact others periodically to check on their job search progress and to see if they know of any job opportunities. Not all students wait until they finish their training to start transcribing—some may already be in business at home or working in an office. Using your network of personal contacts can help you discover job possibilities. Conversely, you can also pass information on job prospects to others, developing two-way relationships for mutual benefit.

JOB SHARING AND COMBINING

Flexibility is one key to success in the changing health care market. If full-time employment is not readily available, job combining may be appropriate. For some people, having two part-time positions may even be preferable to having one full-time job.

Job sharing refers to dividing one full-time (40-hour) transcription position into two half-time (20-hour) positions for two different workers. Benefits may be full, reduced, or not offered, and this should be clearly understood before accepting a job share. Hours of employment and division of responsibilities must also be clear and acceptable to both candidates.

Job combining refers to one individual's obtaining two part-time positions rather than one full-time position. (Of note, both jobs do not have to be transcription positions.) Persons desiring variety or wanting to limit the stress on their hands and wrists from full-time transcribing may elect to take one part-time transcription job and one part-time position in an unrelated field. This option may be temporary, until a full-time position is obtained, or permanent, by individual preference. If possible, at least one position should include adequate benefits. One drawback to this arrangement is that salaries for part-time positions may be lower, hour for hour, than those for full-time jobs.

However, because transcription offers the possibility of working either part-time or full-time, job combining may be a viable option for some. As with full-time positions, basic rules of thumb still apply (reasonable location, adequate wages, environmental standards, and so on). With two positions, two sets of coworkers must be interacted with. At the same time, working half-time in any one office reduces the stresses that come with full-time interaction.

BUSINESS CREATION

In addition to working for others, transcriptionists have the option of starting their own business. Although a year of transcription experience is recommended prior to pursuing self-employment, some new graduates elect to create a transcription business fresh out of school. Creating a business is a complex undertaking; however, if self-employment is the definite career choice, beginning as soon as possible may be a more rapid path toward long-term success. Working part-time in a regular transcription office while growing one's business at home can provide a combination of formal office experience and self-employment.

JOB FAIRS

The concept of a "hiring fair" dates as far back as the Middle Ages. Job fairs, both general and health-care oriented, provide an opportunity for candidates to meet a substantial number of employers in one or two days. You can, and should, attend job fairs while you are still completing your medical transcription coursework. Consider general as well as health care fairs, since general exhibitions may include major health care providers with transcription opportunities.

Attending a job fair requires preparation. Wear appropriate business attire. Bring multiple copies (20–50) of a current resume, personal business cards, and a pocket notebook and pen to keep track of contacts. Select the booths most likely to have transcription or other health care positions. Be prepared to introduce yourself; discuss your qualifications and schooling; collect literature, business cards, and e-mail addresses; and ask for follow-up appointments with interesting employers. After the job fair, contact likely prospects with a brief letter expressing your interest in a transcription position at their institution. File job fair literature where it can be easily retrieved and studied before subsequent job interviews.

TEMPORARY EMPLOYMENT

Temporary agencies have expanded their role far beyond general clerical work and unskilled labor. Both general and medical temporary agencies now exist, and sometimes they place transcriptionists. Some temporary agencies also provide computer training, which might improve your employability. Obtaining temporary employment may help pay for an extended hunt for a permanent transcription position. It may also provide entry into an organization and lead to a permanent position. Also, temporary employment as a transcriptionist, if obtainable, provides legitimate work experience.

Of note, excellent skills will be required by temporary agencies in lieu of work experience. However, temporary work remains a viable path into the mainstream, if permanent employment is difficult to obtain upon graduation. Temporary employment agencies may be listed under "Employment Contractors—Temporary Help" in the Yellow Pages. Some may charge fees for their services, and contracts should be carefully read.

JOB-SCREENING AGENCIES

Job-screening agencies are a new factor in searching for employment. Unlike employment agencies, which can charge the job applicant a substantial fee, job-screening agencies charge employers for providing a list of suitable, prescreened candidates. Applicants are placed into a computer data-base by the screening agency. That data-base is reviewed to find candidates who most closely match an employer's requirements. Job-screening agencies may be found at large job fairs or under "Employment Agencies" in the Yellow Pages.

THE YELLOW PAGES

Many companies provide or require medical transcription services and may have work available even if they are not specifically advertising transcription positions. Review the index at the back of the Yellow Pages for possible transcription employers. These may be listed under the following subject headings: "Chiropractors," "Clinics," "Clinics—Medical," "Dentists," "Employment Agencies," "Employment Contractors—Temporary Help," "Health Care Plans," "Health Care Management," "Home Health Services," "Hospitals," "Laboratories—Medical," "Medical Record Service," "Medical Research & Development," "Medical Transcription," "Mental Health Services," "Midwives," "Nurses," "Nursing Homes," "Nutritionists," "Occupational Therapists," "Physical Therapists," "Physicians" (and many subheadings), "Psychiatrists," "Psychologists," "Secretarial Services," "Transcription," "Typing Service," and "Veterinarians."

WORD OF MOUTH

Even in a large city, each profession seems to develop its own small community. Getting to know experienced medical transcriptionists at AAMT meetings and lectures and tapping their knowledge of the medical community can facilitate your job search. Likewise, informing friends, relatives, and your own health care providers of your desire for a medical transcription position adds to the number of persons actively aware of your job search. A friendly reminder once a month to personal contacts would not be inappropriate.

THE INTERNET

The Internet, and in particular the World Wide Web, is a new and powerful tool for job applicants and employers. The Web provides job hunters with the opportunity to research scores of employers, review job openings in different fields and cities, and post on-line resumes. It allows employers to post open positions on their Web sites. The MT Daily site (http://www.mtdaily.com) is a good starting point for transcription applicants. Web sites of local medical employers may also be of value.

Each aforementioned strategy is a possible route toward employment. The key to becoming a successful transcriptionist is to understand the concept of *service*. Medical transcription is a service industry: transcriptionists serve patients, who rely on them to produce accurate medical records, as well as the institutions and health care providers that employ them. Accuracy, speed, attention to detail, confidentiality, and understanding of medical terminology are the cornerstones of the service provided. The successful job applicant, once hired, will serve the needs of a transcription department with care, flexibility, and enthusiasm. Excellent service is the hallmark of the professional medical transcriptionist.

REVIEW QUESTIONS

1. What is the purpose of a trial offer for a transcription position?
2. How does "piggybacking" work?
3. How much transcription experience is recommended prior to pursuing full-time self-employment?
4. What are the benefits of an internship?
5. What is a lateral transfer?
6. What preparation is required for attending a job fair?

RELATED WEB SITES

WHAT COLOR IS YOUR PARACHUTE: JOB HUNTING ONLINE: http://www.tenspeedpress.com/parachute/front.htm

CAREER CENTER RESOURCES: http://www.monsterboard.com.au/careerc/resource.htm

JOB FAIR SUCCESS: http://www.collegegrad.com/book/11-0.shtml

5
Resumes and Cover Letters

LEARNING OBJECTIVES

- Explain the importance of a resume as a sales tool
- Describe the proper appearance for a professional resume
- Discuss how to present medical transcription coursework on a resume
- Describe the elements of a successful cover letter to a transcription supervisor
- Describe the elements of a successful follow-up letter to a transcription supervisor

ON-THE-JOB PROFILE
Resume Review

When I was a transcription instructor at a technical college, one course requirement for my students was to submit a resume. This was usually done in the last quarter of our one-year program. My class had approximately 30 students, ranging in age from middle 20s up to 62. When I first started teaching, I wrongly assumed that most of my students would have polished, professional resumes all ready to go and that my "guidance" would be a mere formality.

Instead, I found there were three completely different types of students. About a third were quite experienced in compiling resumes and had no problems with it. They didn't need (or particularly want) much help with this aspect of their job hunt, except for how best to present their current education. These students, however, were in the minority.

My second group of students were people who had no professional experience and had worked mainly at low-paying jobs, often for years. To them, medical transcription was a light at the end of a dark tunnel—a way out of chronic financial difficulties. Often this was their first resume, and some were embarrassed to think of putting jobs at fast-food restaurants down as their only work experience. I had to walk them through the process, from rough draft to finished product, and show them how to emphasize their current extensive training and to feel

ON-THE-JOB PROFILE (continued)

good about their work history. When there was little to go on in terms of work experience, we played up their computer or typing skills and their personal qualities, or we switched to a larger typeface to take up more space.

My third group of students were women returning to the workforce after a long absence. Some were homemakers driven to seek employment by economic necessity or a desire for a better standard of living. Others had been away from the professional world for a number of years, had missed the "computer revolution," and were astonished at how much had changed in the last decade. With these students I had to go slowly, easing them back into the working world, reminding them that the abilities they had already developed were still intact. With encouragement, they were able to draw upon their life experiences and create effective resumes.

Although a resume is basically a simple, straightforward presentation of credentials, it was an unfamiliar and even intimidating document to many students. I think "blowing one's own horn" goes against many people's nature. My hardest job was not explaining the resume-making process but convincing my students that it was all right to sell themselves and assertively go after the jobs they wanted and deserved!

A resume is an important tool for conveying a job applicant's experience and qualifications to a prospective employer. In larger health care institutions, where applications are filed with a human resources office, a resume may provide a first impression before any personal contact has been established with the transcription supervisor. A clear, well-presented, professional resume suggests a professional worker.

For the newly trained transcriptionist, work experience may be limited or nonexistent. However, all relevant education and related experience can be presented to make the best possible impression. Taking the time to organize and compose an effective resume will be a good investment in preparing for suitable employment. If desired, consult a professional resume service. Your resume should be no longer than one page, respecting the transcription supervisor's valuable time.

Creating an outline, or rough draft, is the first step in resume preparation. This should include your name, address, and phone number; education; work experience; computer skills; professional affiliations; and personal interests.

In the Education category, include high school; college credit hours completed, if any; and transcription coursework, with expected date of completion. Detail the transcription courses, which might include anatomy and physiology, medical terminology, or pharmacology as well as actual transcription. List specialties transcribed and hours of transcription completed. Include any special clerical or computer training that might assist in transcription.

In the Work Experience category, list your most recent employment first. State the job title, the dates of employment, and the most important duties for each position. Write a brief description of job duties, emphasizing achievements, accomplishments, and major tasks. Be honest but positive. Include contact phone numbers for prior employers.

In the Computer Skills category, list the operating systems (such as Windows 95 or 98) and word processing programs (such as Microsoft Word or Corel WordPerfect) you are familiar with. Include any other computer skills you have, including knowledge of the Internet. Be specific and thorough. Employers realize that knowledge of various computer systems may help a working transcriptionist adapt more readily to inevitable upgrades and changes. Also, many offices still employ older systems and programs, such as DOS, Windows 3.1, and WordPerfect 5.1. Knowledge of these seemingly outdated programs may have value to individual employers.

In the Professional Affiliations category, list relevant memberships, such as AAMT student or professional membership.

In the Personal Interests category, if space permits, list hobbies or interests. These can be as general as reading and hiking; however, unusual or community service activities are more likely to catch a supervisor's eye. Foreign language skills may also be included here.

Once you have finished your first draft, type up a sample resume. If you are working on a home computer, use larger or boldface type for the headings. Revise as needed for clarity. Proofread the entire document with care, as this will help reduce errors in the final draft. Show copies of the preliminary resume to knowledgeable associates, such as transcription or other instructors, and request their input. Consider all comments carefully.

In some resume formats, work experience is listed before education; however, if transcription experience is lacking, then transcription coursework is the more relevant information and should be presented first.

Once you have obtained several critiques, consider additions and corrections as appropriate. Keep in mind that the object is to present an accurate yet very positive summary of your qualifications. The resume is a sales tool, much like a brochure for a product. It introduces the job applicant, and its primary purpose is to motivate the supervisor to request a personal interview.

The level of quality, in terms of the resume's appearance, should be competitive with resumes from other candidates. Paper should be of the highest quality; white or near-white (such as ivory) is recommended. Print enough copies of your resume (one or two hundred) to allow distribution at job fairs and to individual employers. Keep a number of paper copies on file, and also keep your resume on disk or on your hard drive for future reference and updates.

Once you have completed your final draft, proofread it several times—and have one or two other people proofread it as well—to eliminate all typos and other errors. Because accuracy is so vital in medical transcription, an inaccurate resume—even a small typo—could discourage an employer from granting an interview. Be sure that the headings stand out and are easily readable, that the text is tightly written and relevant, and that all applicable job skills (such as typing speed and computer knowledge) have been included.

When your final draft is finished, read it over as though you were a supervisor considering hiring this applicant. Does the language attract your interest? Is the information provided complete, and does it present the best possible picture? Do the paper quality, typefaces, and overall style of the resume generate a professional appearance?

You can use the sample resumes in this chapter (see the accompanying boxes) as examples and as models for general form, style, and presentation of information. However, your actual resume must be in your own words to present an accurate picture of your skills and accomplishments.

MODEL RESUME A

Mary M. Scott
1920 Eagle Rock Rd.
Seattle, WA 98450
206-555-5555

EMPLOYMENT HISTORY:
1998–1999. Medical Transcriptionist, Puget Sound Clinic. Transcription of medical chart notes, medical letters, allied health reports, and specialty dictations in orthopedics and internal medicine. Quality assurance of coworkers' dictations. Incentive pay for high production after first six months.

1995–1996. Retail Clerk, Elegance Fashions. Customer assistance and sales in major mall.

EDUCATION:
Seattle Community College. Medical Transcription Certificate, 1997. Coursework included anatomy and physiology, medical terminology, and SUM dictation series, regular and advanced.

Chief Seattle High School. Graduated 1995. Honor Society member.

COMPUTER SKILLS:
Windows 95, 98, WordPerfect 5.1, home Internet access. Course in Web page design at Lake Washington Business College.

PERSONAL:
Hobbies include cycling, doing crossword puzzles, and reading.
Fluent in Spanish. Familiar with Greek and Latin roots.

MODEL RESUME B

John T. Mason
14402 8th Ave.
Seattle, WA 98155
206-555-1234

EMPLOYMENT HISTORY:

1995–1997   Medical Records Clerk, Ballard Hospital. Assisted in records
              retrieval and distribution, terminal digit system.

1992–1995   Library assistant, Northwest Library. Included on-line searching
              and patron reference assistance, weekend shift.

EDUCATION:

1998–1999   Medical Transcription program, Evergreen Technical College.
              Included A&P and terminology, plus three-month internship at
              Statim Dictation Services.

COMPUTER SKILLS:

Microsoft Windows 95 and 98 operating systems, Medline, and Word Perfect 5.1,
6.0, and 7.0. Basic programming.

PERSONAL:

High school Latin. Hobbies include windsurfing, home computing, hiking.

TAILORING A RESUME

In addition to drafting a general resume that will be appropriate for most medical transcription positions, you can create an individual, or "tailored," resume for a specific job.
This requires researching important characteristics of an institution or employer and
then presenting the facts in a way that more closely matches that employer's needs.

For example, if you are applying to an orthopedic rather than a multispecialty
clinic, find out the types of orthopedics practiced there: sports medicine? general orthopedics? specialization in such areas as shoulder or knee injuries? Once you have obtained this knowledge, review your personal history for individual, educational, or occupational experience that might have specific relevance to this practice. This might
include an allied health position that handled some orthopedic activity, a course in

anatomy with emphasis on bones and joints, or personal experience with sports-related injuries and subsequent rehabilitation.

If a relevant connection can be established, add this information to your resume. Even minor tailoring of this type demonstrates effort expended in researching the facility.

TRANSCRIBING FOR A UNIVERSITY MEDICAL CENTER

Bronwen Taylor

I've been working as a medical transcriptionist since 1973, and I think I've worked in every type of transcription workplace. I've worked at home for myself, on-site for transcription services of several sizes, in a physician's office, for a small hospital, at a medium-sized medical center, and in radiology and pathology departments. Of all environments, my favorite is the large university medical center, where everything is larger than life. The frustrations are greater, but so are the rewards.

Challenge is why I like major medical centers. It was a major challenge to prepare myself to work in such an institution. One has to be at the top of one's game, up to date with every specialty. As it's not possible to know all of this, part of the challenge is to teach yourself how to learn quickly. To start, acquire an effective set of reference tools. English language and listening skills need to be honed, as world-class institutions attract erudite physicians from around the globe. An international staff demands techniques for decoding difficult accents. The basic "trick" is solid familiarity with what is likely to be dictated.

A second challenge of university work is to develop patience. Large institutions can seem cold and impersonal, and nothing happens quickly. The number of skilled transcriptionists using complex software and networks—seemingly effortlessly—will test any new employee's resolve during training. One has to take it on faith that things will eventually make sense. On the plus side, large institutions can offer very good benefit packages, and they are probably among the most secure positions an MT can have.

In the university environment, certain terms will be difficult to find, because when the dictator first says them, it's the first time they've been *said*, period. Oncology divisions, for example, use experimental protocols full of terms found only in specialty journals or even just in letters from one physician to another.

As in every MT environment, productivity is measured, and little allowance is made for the complexity of the work. To meet the quota one has to work consistently. This, of course, applies to transcription wherever it's done. Learning to do this means learning to use reference material and get back to the keyboard quickly. Long breaks for chatting are a thing of the past in today's MT environment.

There are two particularly rewarding aspects to working at a large medical center. The first is that patients are, for the most part, seriously ill and need

TRANSCRIBING FOR A UNIVERSITY MEDICAL CENTER (continued)

help. It's gratifying to be a part, if a tiny part, of a team working to provide that help. Second, opportunities for continuing education are so vast in this job that it almost makes one dizzy. The reports themselves teach. With a little more effort, the university campus and library yield a whole world of videotapes and lectures. In short, the variety and complexity of the work is why I love working at a university medical center.

THE ON-LINE RESUME

The sudden and massive expansion of Internet use in the last few years has created an entirely new arena for job hunters. Access to on-line job opportunities is not limited to home computer owners. Internet access may also be available at local public libraries, college and university libraries, copy shops, computer stores, and even cafes providing Internet services to customers. Posting a resume on the World Wide Web and accessing the many job-related databases now available is a new and ever-expanding tool for researching and possibly obtaining employment.

The equipment required to go on-line at home includes a computer, with preferably a Pentium or equivalent processor chip; a modem capable of at least a 28,800 baud (or bps, for bits per second) connection rate; a telephone line; and an ISP, or Internet service provider. The ISP can be a well-known national service such as America Online, which provides full Internet access as well as proprietary content, or a local company that offers Internet access only. Faster modems capable of connecting at 56,000 baud or even better allow swifter transfer of information and are recommended. You can also access the Internet at your local public library or on computers rented by the hour. Librarians may provide instruction on how to use Web browsers, such as Netscape's Navigator and Microsoft's Internet Explorer.

On-line resumes may be submitted in what is called ASCII format (American Standard Code for Information Interchange). This is a basic text-only file format that is often used for e-mail. Web sites such as careermosaic.com require this. Other Web sites, such as monster.com, allow copy and paste techniques on standard word processing files. Instructions and assistance will be available on individual Web sites.

If you are submitting an application form on-line, you can use "cut and paste" techniques to transfer information from your resume to an on-line form, you can retype the information directly onto the on-line form, or you may be able to send or attach an "e-mail resume" with the application form.

THE COVER LETTER

Like a good resume, an effective cover letter to an employer is a tool for explaining and clarifying your credentials. It also personalizes the interaction more than a resume does, allowing a warmer and more human contact. For best results, each cover letter should be unique to the specific job applied for and person contacted.

The elements of a successful cover letter are as follows:

1. *The heading.* Include the current date; your name, address, and phone number, the contact person's name and job title; and the employer's company name and address.
2. *The greeting.* For example, "Dear Ms. Preston:"
3. *The first paragraph.* Explain the reason for the cover letter, name the specific position you are applying for, and mention if you were referred or recommended by a person known to the employer.
4. *The second paragraph.* In this paragraph, summarize qualifications of interest to the employer that distinguish you from other candidates and/or make you especially suited to the job.
5. *The third and final paragraph.* In this paragraph, reiterate your strong interest in the advertised position, thank the employer for his or her time, and, if desired, say that you will make a follow-up call on a specific date to ensure that the mailed resume and application were received (this not only demonstrates your strong interest in the job but also is proactive and is preferable to waiting for the employer to call you).

A cover letter should be brief (no longer than one page), concise, and positive. For a letter from a medical transcription student who is nearing graduation or who has just completed training, the first paragraph should express a strong interest in entering the profession and should also explain why the specific position being applied for is so attractive and appropriate.

If you do not yet have transcription work experience, emphasize in the second paragraph the transcription coursework you have completed, subjects (such as medical terminology or anatomy and physiology) you have studied, and classroom hours you have put in. Include word processing skills, an excellent typing speed, and related work experience or job skills (such as medical reference ability, medical records employment, or even medical searching on the Internet).

For the concluding paragraph, stress the enthusiasm of a new transcriptionist and your appreciation for any opportunity to work and learn in a professional environment. Be very positive, yet genuine. The accompanying model cover letter (see box) illustrates these concepts.

MODEL COVER LETTER

October 12, 1999

Mary M. Scott
1920 Eagle Rock Rd.
Seattle, WA 98450

Adele Johns, Transcription Supervisor
Statim Medical Clinic
240 63rd St. NE
Seattle, WA 98334

Dear Ms. Johns:

My medical transcription instructor, Mr. Edward Wilkes, suggested I apply for the transcription position you advertised in the Sunday *Seattle Times*. As a newly graduated transcriptionist, I am greatly interested in the opportunity to work at Statim Medical Clinic and feel I could serve your patients and providers well.

In addition to completing a one-year course in medical transcription, with separate coursework in anatomy and basic pharmacology, I have prior work experience in medical billing at St. John's Hospital and a lifelong interest in the health care field. I am quite familiar with word processing programs such as WordPerfect 5.1 and have used Medline and other medical sites on the World Wide Web.

Thank you for considering my application for the position of medical transcriptionist. I look forward to meeting you and will call next week to make sure my application was received and to answer any additional questions you may have.

Sincerely,

Mary M. Scott

There are several points worth noting about this sample cover letter. The first is that Ms. Scott refers to herself as a "newly graduated transcriptionist" rather than as a transcription student. This establishes her as a professional rather than a student.

Next, Ms. Scott mentions her prior work experience in medical billing. Any work experience in the health care field may interest an employer, and mentioning this experience lends credibility to her claim of a lifelong interest in the health professions. Also, mentioning her word processing skills and computer/Internet activities suggests that extensive training in those areas will not be necessary—a plus for the busy transcription supervisor.

The offer to phone a week later and answer further questions gives the supervisor time to formulate questions and consider the resume and application package. When phoning, basic courtesy ("Is this a good time to talk?" or "Do you have a minute to discuss my application packet?") is essential to respect the transcription supervisor's needs.

Unlike the cover letter, which is fairly standard, a follow-up letter seems to be a "rare bird." For this reason, a follow-up letter of thanks for a personal interview may have even more weight than a cover letter does. Within one or two days after a personal interview, compose a brief follow-up letter that mentions the position desired and sincerely thanks the interviewer for his or her time. Be brief and courteous, and do not ask for any additional favors or assistance. Mail the follow-up letter promptly.

A sample follow-up letter is included in the accompanying box.

MODEL FOLLOW-UP LETTER

October 22, 1999

Mary M. Scott
1920 Eagle Rock Rd.
Seattle, WA 98450

Adele Johns, Transcription Supervisor
Statim Medical Clinic
240 63rd St. NE
Seattle, WA 98334

Dear Ms. Johns:

It was so nice to meet you today at the Statim Medical Clinic. I just wanted to take a moment to thank you again for the interview. I'm excited about the prospect of working with you as a medical transcriptionist, and really appreciate your time and consideration. If any further information is required, please let me know.

Sincerely,

Mary M. Scott

A personal, individualized letter should follow every job interview, not only as a courtesy but also because of human nature. Supervisors want more than just the best transcriptionists available; they want the best *people*—people who will get along with their existing employees, become team players, and make the work environment more pleasant. A person considerate enough to write a letter of thanks is likely to be a positive addition to a transcription office.

Keep careful records of applications filed or mailed, interviews, and follow-up letters and calls. This will help coordinate the job search process and avoid duplication of effort or missed opportunities. Similarly, requesting e-mail addresses may add another avenue for communication and professional interaction.

 ON-THE-JOB PROFILE

Following Up

My first lesson in the importance of following up came when, as a very young man, I applied for a ward clerk position in the 1970s. My mother already worked at a medical center, and she had encouraged me to apply and take the test for admission to the ward clerk training class. I took the test, thought I had done well, and waited patiently for the phone call announcing my admission.

Days passed. Two weeks passed.

On the morning of the deadline, my mom phoned me from work.

"Did they call you about the job yet?"

"Not yet."

I heard a snort on the other end of the phone.

"We'll see about that!"

Fifteen minutes later I received a call from the head of personnel (the archaic term for human resources).

"Mr. Drake? Oh, yes, you're in the class. In fact, you had the highest score on the test. We just misplaced your application. Sorry."

They misplaced my application.

They were sorry.

If my mother hadn't followed up on that, my medical career might never have begun.

The value of following up again hit home some years later, this time from the opposite perspective. By then I was managing a medical library and had a position open for a library assistant. Nine qualified candidates applied for the job. All had respectable credentials. All interviewed reasonably well. It would have been a difficult decision, except for one small thing . . . .

One of the nine applicants wrote me a thank-you letter. She said how much she liked the looks of "my" library and that she knew she would enjoy working there.

Nine qualified applicants. One thank-you note.

Is there any question who got the job?

REVIEW QUESTIONS

1. Why is knowledge of different word processing systems valuable to employers?
2. Should only one person proofread your resume?
3. What is an on-line resume?
4. What relevant skills might be worth including in a cover letter to a transcription supervisor?
5. Why might a follow-up letter be preferable to an unscheduled visit or phone call?

RELATED WEB SITES

TIPS ON RESUME WRITING: http://www.montana.edu/wwwcp/tips.html

JOBSMART HOME: http://www.jobsmart.org/tools/resume/index.htm

RESUMECM: http://www.careermosaic.com/cm/cm39.html

PREPARING A RESUME: http://www.rpi.edu/dept/llc/writecenter/web/text/resume.html

RESUME CONNECTION: http://www.careerpath.com/ows~bin/aux/register

PREPARING YOUR RESUME FOR THE INTERNET: http://www.dbm.com/nbgu/de/resume.html

200 LETTERS FOR JOB HUNTERS: http://www.careerlab.com/letters/default.htm

CAREER CITY COVER LETTERS: http://www.careercity.com/content/cvlttr/

40 FREE ONLINE RESUME AND JOB SEARCH WORKSHOPS: http://www.provenresumes.com/

PREPARING A COVER LETTER: http://www.rpi.edu/dept/llc/writecenter/web/text/coverltr.html

6
Negotiating the Job Offer

LEARNING OBJECTIVES

- Explain the long-term importance of obtaining a higher starting salary
- Discuss how a benefits package enhances the actual salary
- Describe ways to compare and contrast different job offers
- Explain the importance of engaging in mutually beneficial, "win-win" negotiation

ON-THE-JOB PROFILE
Win-Win Negotiations

The purpose of negotiation is to bring two parties together, establish communications, and provide a mutually satisfactory outcome. You may not get everything you want, but you should get an acceptable result—as should the other party.

I've often asked myself, what does it take to be a successful negotiator? In dealings with my family and business partners, I find preparation is one key to a good result. I have to know exactly what I want and the reasons why I should get it. The more I can clearly define and support my position and express why my outcome will improve conditions for the other party as well, the better chance I have of reaching my goals. If I don't prepare and just haphazardly enter into negotiations, the outcome is much less predictable and positive.

In my own family, this has worked well in meetings with my wife and teenage stepson. A teenager doesn't want to be ordered about—he wants to know the reasons why things have to be a certain way. If the reasons are convincing enough, agreement is more likely. In financial matters, if written documentation is also provided to support one's decisions, then the chances of reaching an amicable settlement seem to increase greatly. Planning and documentation also show the other party that he or she is worth taking the time to prepare for.

A second key component in negotiation is empathy—seeing the other person's side of the question. Most people have reasons for their desires and behaviors.

ON-THE-JOB PROFILE (continued)

Finding those reasons can help produce a beneficial and permanently acceptable result. Also, what seems obvious and logical to one person may be baffling or unreasonable to another. That doesn't mean either party is right or wrong; it just means perceptions and life experience differ, and compromise may be necessary to achieve a final resolution.

The classic concept of "win-win" negotiation seems the best way to approach job offers, requests for a raise, and grievances or disputes. Before stating his or her case, the employee should consider what the organization needs at present, if coworkers will be affected, and how to make the desired personal outcome also benefit the group. For example, changing from an evening shift to a more desirable day shift might involve offering to work one weekend a month to help with coverage. (After all, if you get what you want, why shouldn't everyone else?) And requesting a raise should certainly be preceded by compiling all production and quality statistics, to document that additional value is already being provided to the company.

During a personal interview, a transcription supervisor may ask for your desired salary requirement or range, benefits, and preferred hours of employment. The supervisor may also mention the organizational pay scale, any probationary period, and levels of employment, such as Transcriptionist I or Transcriptionist II. A knowledge of local pay rates at comparable organizations is helpful in determining whether an offered salary is satisfactory. Remember that the first offer may not be the best possible offer and that a new graduate is more likely to be offered a salary at the lower end of the pay scale than one at the upper end.

After the transcription supervisor has finished interviewing and considering candidates, he or she may extend an offer of employment. This offer should be carefully evaluated before acceptance, as one's starting point often determines one's destination.

For example, the supervisor might offer an entry-level salary to a new transcriptionist. However, the supervisor might have discretion to exceed that salary for an exceptional candidate. Once a person is hired, his or her future pay raises will be based on a percentage of the starting salary—therefore, the higher the starting salary, the higher the subsequent raises. For example, a 3 percent raise on $10 an hour would equal 30 cents per hour, but a 3 percent raise on $12 an hour would equal 36 cents per hour, and each year that advantage would increase.

An additional important factor to consider when negotiating your starting salary is the "hidden" costs of benefits and the portion taken out for taxes. Many health and dental plans require partial payments by the employee, for example. State employers, such as state university hospitals, may also have a mandatory teacher's-type retirement plan that takes an additional percentage of one's gross salary. Add to this money taken by federal, Social Security, state, and Medicaid taxes, and payroll deductions may exceed 25 percent or even 30 percent of gross income. This means a $10 hourly salary may only bring home $7.00 to $7.50 per hour.

However, the intrinsic value of included benefits should be considered an addition to salary. An employer offering medical and dental benefits, vacation, sick leave, and a retirement plan adds considerably to the basic salary. If you receive several similar job offers, comparing levels of benefits as well as salaries may make a deciding difference. Consider as well employer contributions to pension plans, any profit-sharing or stock options, and educational or professional development benefits.

PROFESSIONALISM IN THE WORKPLACE

Marcy Diehl

At the end of every document that you transcribe, you type your initials. What do these initials say?

You tell me.

Now I will tell you what I think they should say. They should say: "This is *my* work, and I am proud of it. I did the best I could. I was careful to record exactly what the dictator said, yet I made it read better if there were any inadvertent errors in the material. I wanted the document to look good, sound good, print out perfectly, and be medically and grammatically sound. I checked to be sure that I had the patient's name and any demographic material concerning that patient correct in every way. I avoided unnecessary use of abbreviations or shortcuts that might confuse any reader of this document. I carefully spell-checked and proofread the document. No words were guessed at. Blanks with notes were attached when there was any doubt about the accuracy of the material. I did not discuss any part of this document with any person not concerned with its production or development. I made sure it was safe and properly distributed to the correct channels for its security. I did not discuss the dictator or the habits of the dictator at any time."

To be secure about myself when I affix my signature (my initials), I make sure I am doing the best of which I am capable. I belong to my professional organization, attend meetings, support and participate in its activities. I encourage others in my field to join in, and I assist and mentor newcomers. I share new things that I learn that will help others with their production or quality of their work. I admit, however, that I don't know everything, and I remember to give credit to those who have assisted me. I know what I am doing and that I am doing it well. I have achieved the education I feel is necessary to be successful in my field, and I continue to seek out methods to continue this education. I am fun and dependable to work with, and I keep my commitments to those who may request my services as well as to fellow practitioners. I truly like myself and am true to myself. I adapt to changes in my field and try to be aware of these changes quickly.

I network with other professionals and look for opportunities to learn from them, teach them, respect them, and make them look good. I charge fairly for my

PROFESSIONALISM IN THE WORKPLACE (continued)

services and I pay wages fairly to those whom I employ. I do my work quickly but carefully. I dispose of or store any notes or parts of records that are not required, in a safe and secure manner. I look, act, and dress like a professional whenever I am in the public view. I understand medical ethics and am aware of the nature of the medical-legal aspects concerning medical records. I am unfailingly honest about reporting lines completed, hours worked, and materials used.

Why?

Because I want to be able to truthfully report that I am a professional medical transcriptionist.

After thoroughly evaluating a job offer, a prospective employee can enter into negotiation at the time of hiring. Negotiation is an expression of requests, not demands, designed to adjust the job offer to satisfy the needs of both the applicant and the employer. It should be undertaken with the goal of achieving a mutually beneficial, "win-win" result that will contribute to a long-term, positive working relationship between the two parties.

If the salary offer is inadequate, address this issue at the time of hire, prior to signing contracts. Request a more desirable figure, offering reasons to support your request. If a previous salary was as high or even higher than the offered salary, mention this fact, as a baseline wage has previously been established.

Flexibility is important in negotiation, as is listening to the employer's rationale for the salary offered. An unacceptable offer can still be declined; however, the salary must be considered in terms of the overall wage and benefits package, job location and work hours, local job availability, and the applicant's current financial situation.

Hours of employment may also be negotiable. Having specific work hours in mind makes sense, but so does adaptability to an employer's scheduling needs. If night or weekend coverage is required, ask if a rotation is possible, rather than agreeing, as the newest employee, to cover every weekend. Work out child care or family concerns before signing a contract.

In regard to benefits, find out if they start immediately or if there is a 30-, 60-, or even 90-day waiting period before benefits commence. It may or may not be possible to reduce or eliminate such a waiting period through negotiation; this will depend on whether the supervisor is authorized to adjust the waiting period and how eager the organization is to hire you. It should be mentioned that any negotiation should not be undertaken casually but with a good reason, such as economic or personal hardship, that can be clearly explained to the hiring supervisor.

Once an offer is made and accepted, careful documentation and filing of all agreements is advised. The date of hire, in particular, will often be referred to later on. The terms of employment, including wages, benefits, and working hours, need to be spelled out and retained. A complete job description should be requested, and an employee handbook if available. Reserve a section of your personal files at home for job-related materials.

When you get your first paycheck, check the hourly wage, taxes taken out, and all other deductions for accuracy. File all pay stubs for a cumulative record of income. Also, study and then file benefits information for easy retrieval. Maintaining excellent files will allow easy access to your employee benefit data. A semiannual review of your job benefits may improve your utilization of them. Also, if pension plans require a year's employment before initiation, keep the date of hire in mind so you can request pension activation at the earliest possible time.

The accompanying box provides a sample negotiation scenario.

SAMPLE JOB NEGOTIATION

APPLICANT:	Good morning, Ms. Davis.
SUPERVISOR:	Good morning, Ms. Scott. I'd like to make you an offer of employment, as we discussed on the phone yesterday.
APPLICANT:	That's wonderful! I've been job hunting for several weeks now, but Statim Medical was definitely my first choice.
SUPERVISOR:	I'm glad to hear that. Now, the salary that I mentioned was $12.50 to start, with a 50-cent-per-hour raise after six months. Does that sound about right?
APPLICANT:	Well, I know this is my first professional position, and I don't expect to start at the top of the pay scale. However, my last position before my transcription training paid $13.50 per hour.
SUPERVISOR:	Yes, but you said that was a contract position without benefits. I don't think that's comparable to what we're offering.
APPLICANT:	No, you're quite right, and I feel a little uncomfortable asking you for $13.50. But my cost of living has gone up substantially since that position. If there's any way I could get a higher wage, it would take a lot of pressure off me.
SUPERVISOR:	I understand that prices have risen.
APPLICANT:	Also, and this may sound self-serving, but all my future raises will be percentages of my initial salary, won't they?
SUPERVISOR:	That's our current practice.
APPLICANT:	That means if I start too low, it limits my earnings from now on.
SUPERVISOR:	I know what you mean. As the transcription supervisor, I have some flexibility in setting wages. I could bring you in at $13, with a 50-cent raise guaranteed after successful completion of your six-month probationary period. I'm afraid subsequent raises would only be based on the $13, but that's the best I can do in our system.
APPLICANT:	Thank you! That's more than fair.
SUPERVISOR:	You're welcome. I look forward to working with you.

Like most successful negotiations, the goal is for both parties to be satisfied with the outcome and eager to work together. Both give and take are required to negotiate an acceptable agreement. Learning more about organizational policies, through listening and careful questioning during the interview, may improve your overall satisfaction with the results.

Although no job will have all desired qualities in one package, many positions can provide a satisfactory start in transcription, with financial and personal benefits expanding over time. Skillful negotiating will not only help you obtain appropriate wages and benefits, it will also demonstrate to your employer that you are a careful and knowledgeable professional worthy of respect.

REVIEW QUESTIONS

1. What techniques could be used to overcome an unacceptably low salary offer?
2. How does the level of benefits affect a salary offer?
3. Should negotiation of benefits or salary be undertaken casually?
4. What types of documentation should be kept upon acceptance of an offer of employment?
5. How does an unacceptably low wage affect future earnings?
6. What are the hidden costs of employee benefits?

RELATED WEB SITES

SALARY NEGOTIATIONS: http://www.me.washington.edu/ug/jobs/salary.html

CAREER PLANNING AND RELOCATION RESOURCES: http://www.pohly.com/career.shtml

THE NOEL SMITH-WENKEL SALARY NEGOTIATION METHOD: http://www.nmt.edu/~shipman/org/noel.html

SUCCESSFUL INTERVIEWING: http://www.dac.nev.edu/coop.careerservices/interview.html

7
Hitting the Wall

LEARNING OBJECTIVES

- List several factors that can make it difficult to find a medical transcription position within a reasonable time
- Discuss personal factors that may limit a prospective employee's availability
- Explain options to consider when faced with a difficult job search
- Suggest adjustments to the job-search process to enhance the chances of success

 ON-THE-JOB PROFILE
Challenges of Relocation

After transcribing for four years in Austin, Texas, I moved to Houston, in 1990. The Houston style of hiring was very different from what I later experienced in Seattle. I studied the newspaper my first week in town, chose a clinic, and rode a bus over there. They accepted my application, saying they'd call me in a week or two. However, I couldn't wait, so I checked the papers again and went over to Medifax, a national transcription service I was familiar with.

I walked into the office and asked to speak to the manager. The secretary said the manager was at lunch and asked if I would mind waiting 20 minutes for her to return. I sat down, and the manager arrived shortly thereafter. She took my resume, looked it over, then offered to test me. I agreed. I took a transcription test, checked it, and then handed it to her. She studied the test with a critical eye.

"You got one wrong," she said shortly.

"I know," I replied. "The doctor said the word wrong on the tape."

"Well," she sighed, "I got the same one wrong when I took the test. Where would you like to sit?"

"Over by the windows," I replied. "Monday at eight?"

"We'll see you then."

ON-THE-JOB PROFILE (continued)

That was Texas hiring at its finest. My work in Houston was excellent, transcribing reports for the Texas Medical Center and specialty reports for the Texas Lung Institute.

When I moved to Seattle two years later, I had little idea of the cultural differences that are possible between two cities. Following my usual procedure, I selected several likely locations and went there in person. All were hospitals with personnel offices. All told me the same thing: "We'll take your application, and the supervisor will contact you in two weeks."

"That's it?"

"Yes, Sir. Thank you for coming in."

I was taken aback by the cool formality of Northwesterners. They hadn't even offered me a cup of coffee, much less a transcription test. It was as though I were not a hotshot transcriptionist but just an ordinary *job applicant!*

Two weeks later, like clockwork, the promised postcards arrived:

"Dear Mr. Drake: Thank you for applying for the medical transcription position. We will call you for a transcription test." Just like that. I still hadn't even talked with anyone. Yet, several days later the calls came in, and I was at last summoned for an interview. Since I had spent every penny I had moving to Seattle, I took the first job offered. Luckily, it was at a major hospital, where I continued to learn and grow.

This is just one example of the type of regional differences a relocating transcriptionist might encounter. In any moving situation, the new city will pose a challenge to the medical transcriptionist, whether because of the different culture of the new city or a lack of contacts and associates. *Patience* may become the most significant word in the relocated transcriptionist's lexicon. But whatever state or city you select, *courtesy* and *quality* will certainly be understood.

Even after two to three months of regular, five-days-a-week job hunting, a percentage of applicants still will not have obtained a medical transcription position. After 60 to 90 days, an unsuccessful job hunt needs to be reevaluated. This requires a critical look, not only at the methods used but also at the individual and the community of residence. Several major factors may be considered, including

1. Local job availability
2. Amount of effort expended
3. Competition for available positions
4. Feedback from transcription supervisors
5. Personal limiting factors (working hours, location, child care, and such)
6. Job hunting strategies versus community and individual styles
7. Individual ability and suitability for the medical transcription profession

Local job availability is the first consideration. In smaller communities there may be few MT positions available. Such situations may require either commuting to a nearby community with a higher population, relocating to a larger city, or, possibly, telecommuting. Seasonal variations in local hiring may also have a negative impact, such as in college towns, where hiring is often affected by the academic calendar. For those graduating from transcription programs in December rather than May or June, the holidays and the post-holiday lull may inhibit their search. Also, budgetary considerations related to the unique fiscal years of businesses and institutions may restrict hiring. Transcription managers may prefer, or be required, to wait for the start of the next fiscal year before posting new positions.

An unsuccessful job seeker must also honestly and realistically examine the amount of effort he or she has expended. Although there is no guarantee that extra effort will increase your chances of obtaining a medical transcription position, applying for four jobs per week instead of one or two, or six instead of four, may raise the probability of being hired, if positions are available and other factors are equal.

Review any notes you have taken during your job-seeking process. Did you keep appointments on time? Did you make follow-up calls and mail thank-you notes? Were the positions you applied for appropriate to your qualifications? Did you request referrals to other potential employers?

Consider how many days per week, and how many hours per day, you have actually spent job hunting. Does this represent the best possible effort? Would spending more time or following up more assertively likely produce better results?

Do not underestimate the local competition for transcription positions. In cities with community or technical colleges, classes may graduate students on a quarterly, semiannual, or annual basis into the job market. At the same time, changes in the health care sector of the economy or the economy overall—such as staff cutbacks, wage freezes or cuts, reduced benefits, or less desirable working conditions—may place experienced transcriptionists in the same job pool as new graduates. Employers will be reluctant to discuss the number of applicants for any given position. However, a continued lack of success may be related to an excess of qualified, or more qualified, applicants.

Conversely, the opposite situation can also exist, in which there is more work available than qualified applicants, and an organization's transcription requirements may expand as well as contract. Patience and persistence are the job hunter's best allies.

An unresponsive hiring environment may improve over time.

Feedback from transcription supervisors regarding your qualifications, presentation, and likelihood of success is highly desirable. If declined for a position, it is appropriate to make a brief follow-up call to thank the supervisor for the opportunity to apply and to request suggestions for improvement. Have specific questions written out and on hand to make the most of this call. Ask if factors other than your transcription experience came into play, including your appearance, test scores, resume and background, work history, and education. Request that the organization keep your resume on file, and ask whether a follow-up call in one or two months would be welcome.

In any job hunt, and particularly in tight local labor markets, personal limiting factors may play important or even deciding roles. These can be as simple as an inability to work evenings or weekends, a need to leave work in the early afternoon to take care of child care responsibilities, or an inability to work full-time. Finding ways around such personal limitations, if possible, can demonstrate above-average commitment to a prospective employer. Tolerating a less convenient schedule can not only fill a gap for a supervisor but also can be evidence of your keen desire for the position. However, if you do accept a less-than-desirable schedule, you may want to specify a time limit for reconsidering it, such as six months. Similarly, responsibility for working evening or weekend hours or overtime to accommodate heavy workloads should be shared by all departmental transcriptionists, not just the new hires.

As this chapter's opening profile demonstrates, unfamiliarity with the local culture is another factor that can impede a job hunt. In some regions, assertiveness is valued and appreciated, and a personal visit to a transcription office denotes strong interest. In other areas, formality and discretion rule, and a written application submitted to the human resources office is preferred. Knowledge of local hiring styles, developed during the job-search process, will help prevent lost opportunities.

The final factor to consider in determining the viability of your job-hunting process is your individual ability and suitability for the positions you are applying for. Evaluating this requires frank self-examination. Have you conveyed to the hiring supervisor an ability to transcribe and edit challenging dictations in a timely manner? Is this ability genuine, based on extensive study and practice? Is your transcribing speed adequate? Are your spelling, grammar, medical terminology, and comprehension excellent? Is your knowledge of anatomy, physiology, and basic pharmacology sufficient for an entry-level position?

Consider your suitability as well as your ability. Your suitability relates to your ability to harmonize with the setting and personnel, and your level of comfort with this line of work. Sitting relatively still for eight hours, wearing headphones all day, and concentrating for extended periods of time are necessary characteristics. Accuracy and attention to detail are likewise essential. If multiple supervisors, over a period of months, consistently perceive that you are not suitable for this line of work, then you may need to reevaluate whether this career is indeed appropriate for you, or at least whether you are presenting yourself appropriately.

Once you have hit "the wall," receiving no employment offers for a period of three months, you need to review your options and make some decisions. Your options at this point could include

1. Continuing your current job-search process for an extended time—funding it, if necessary, through loans, family, or savings
2. Adjusting and refining your process
3. Expanding the geographical area of your search or the time spent job hunting
4. Securing professional employment assistance
5. Accepting temporary employment while continuing the process
6. Relocating
7. Postponing or abandoning the job search

ENTERING TRANSCRIPTION

Mark Aguirre

I was 21 years old, selling cars, and things weren't going too well. I ended up being "relieved of duty" one day. I didn't think much of it. I had a car payment to make, rent, and so on, but I always managed to get by.

One morning I woke up—about three months after I had left my job—went outside to leave, and *no car*. It had been repossessed. My bank told me that if I gave them $1,000 by the end of the week they would not report my repossession. How in the world was I going to get $1,000 by Friday?

Now, I had always been a good typist, with the highest grade in my eighth-grade class. My mother was a medical transcriptionist, and she had quite a large account that she ran out of her house. She asked me if I would try to help her; she would pay me. She gave me a pediatrics tape and told me to type what I heard and, if I had a question, to let her know.

I muscled through this tape and had a bunch of questions. I asked her, and she gave me the answers. (My mother is a pretty smart gal.) After I did this for about a day to help her out, she paid me.

Wow, I thought—you are paying me this to do that? Considering that it was only 10 cents a line, I did all right. I couldn't believe this. Everything that I was really good at or really liked to do—typing, computers, and medicine—was all in this job. I began to think that I might have found something here.

After about six months, my mother sold her account to a local company. She didn't need to work, anyway, but she enjoyed it. I went to work for the company she sold the account to, because I knew it fairly well. I was a transcriptionist for a little over two years there and have recently taken over managing that account, and I now run our company's training program. I have about seven people that I teach about our company and "show them the ropes," the same way Mom did for me three years ago.

It's amazing how much you can succeed in your life if you can find what you are really good at. I really do owe Mom one, huh?

Continuing the job-search process for several more months, if financially possible, is a valid course of action if adequate positions in the community appear to be available or likely to open up. If you have invested a significant amount of time in training for the transcription profession, six months or even longer may be a reasonable amount of time to continue searching. Once obtained, a permanent professional position should prove well worth a long preliminary job search.

Adjusting the job-search process may be preferable to simply continuing it. Expanding the hours and/or days you spend hunting; increasing your contacts in the community; requesting personal interviews with career counselors, teachers, ministers, and other knowledgeable and "connected" persons; and generally working both harder and smarter may improve your chances of success. A monthly evaluation of your search process and feedback from employers can help you keep your search on track. Leaving no stone unturned will not only improve your chances, it will also leave you with the feeling that you made every reasonable effort to obtain employment.

Expanding the geographical area of your search and the number of hours per day and days per week spent searching are two other distinct possibilities. This might mean driving farther to work than you would prefer; finding or initiating a car pool; taking an early bus to another community, if available; or even leasing or purchasing a car, if possible, if you are currently limited to public transportation. Also, revising your schedule to allow for evening and weekend work opportunities, and thereby being able to offer the maximum flexibility in a job interview, is an action that may be required by the hard realities of a reluctant marketplace.

Securing professional assistance, from an employment agency, a career counselor, or even a state employment office, may be an as-yet-untraveled avenue for candidates in a reluctant job market. An experienced professional may suggest alternative methods for pursuing the job search and provide additional business contacts. Also, some available positions never make it to the Sunday papers but are listed with career brokers or employment offices instead, for screening purposes.

Accepting temporary employment is one way of financing a protracted job search. However, most temporary clerical positions take place during the standard 8:00 to 5:00 workday, which makes it difficult to job hunt. Full-time temporary work may inhibit a job search, and part-time temporary work is harder to find. But a temporary transcription position, if available, is valuable work experience. A temporary transcription-related position, such as a job in a hospital medical records office, may provide useful contacts. A temporary position for several months may be just what you need in a tight transcription market until conditions improve.

Relocation is a serious and expensive matter. Three unsuccessful months of job hunting is probably insufficient to warrant such a major change. If the local job market is stagnant, a move to a more vital and populous area after six months should not be completely discounted. However, it seems preferable to evaluate your community for job availability while still in school, making sure there are sufficient medical employers to present a good possibility of being hired.

Finally, postponing or abandoning the job-search process is a last resort. Postponing the search indicates a temporary break in activity, due to local or personal conditions. To be successful, it requires setting a specific date for resumption of the job search. Having concrete plans to resume before suspending the search will make this resumption more likely to occur.

Abandoning the job search, if all resources are exhausted, is the final and least desirable option. This may indicate either unsuitability for a career in medical transcription, inability to perform the work at a professional level, an acute scarcity of appropriate jobs locally, reluctance to relocate to a more positive job market, or insufficient experience and computer sophistication to work as a telecommuter.

Considering the time and money invested in a transcriptionist's training, this option should be elected only when all resources have been exhausted or when personal incompatibility with the profession cannot be resolved. A decision of this importance must be discussed with trusted advisers, as others' points of view may provide valuable insights that will help you either resolve the conflict or adopt a more suitable course of action. A final consideration is the fact that changing careers will mean again investing in the expense of schooling and the subsequent job hunt, and there will still be no guarantee of finding employment.

REVIEW QUESTIONS

1. What is "the wall"? What must be done when one "hits the wall" in a job search?
2. What three factors might explain an inability to obtain a medical transcription position within three to six months?
3. What personal factors could adversely affect a person's employability?
4. What personal factors might indicate a person's suitability for a medical transcription position?
5. How would you personally adjust an unsuccessful job search?

RELATED WEB SITES

THE 25 WORST JOB INTERVIEW MISTAKES: http://www.thomas-staffing.com/jobtip1.htm
JOB HUNTING ERRORS TO AVOID: http://www.careerlab.com/art_avoiderrorrs.htm
EIGHT MYTHS ABOUT JOB HUNTING: http://www.job-hunting.com/

8
The First Transcription Job

LEARNING OBJECTIVES

- Name several characteristics of a suitable transcription workstation
- List basic medical reference books that should be kept at the workstation
- Discuss transcription work flow, from dictator through dictation system to transcriptionist
- Explain ways to balance productivity and accuracy

ON-THE-JOB PROFILE
The New Transcriptionist

My first multispecialty transcription job was at a regional clinic in Austin, Texas. I already had some radiology and family practice experience, but I was quite overwhelmed by transcribing for 35 different physicians in a dozen different specialties.

I distinctly remember my first day at work. I would struggle through a difficult report, then sit and rest for five minutes. My total daily count was about two hundred lines; I was stunned to learn that my more experienced colleagues averaged four times that.

Besides having to learn new terminology, I also had to grapple with problems related to dictation style. One dictator seemed terribly disorganized, frequently jumping backwards and forwards. As I was using an electric typewriter—and carbon paper for triplicate copies—this was virtually impossible. Another dictator had very unusual pauses and phrasing but was a stickler for accuracy. It took several months before I could transcribe his reports with confidence.

An additional benefit of this job to my professional development was the pediatrics work the clinic did. In particular, one physician focused on attention deficit disorder, and my knowledge of this difficult condition (and my sympathy for those who experience it) expanded dramatically.

ON-THE-JOB PROFILE   (continued)

The challenge of contending with new specialties was balanced by the joy of learning. I found the diverse clinic reports more interesting than my former diet of chest and shoulder x-rays. Still, I made many obvious mistakes at the start—such as typing W&L (wins and losses?) instead of WNL (within normal limits).

Certainly, every transcriptionist has to start somewhere; no one begins with two years of experience. Finding a good entry-level job—one that informs as well as challenges and provides new understanding of the human condition—is not easy but is by no means impossible. Such a job will be the first step to a rewarding, profitable, and personally satisfying career.

Beginning a new position, as well as a new career, is both exciting and intimidating. There is much to learn about job duties specific to the organization, the practical process of medical transcription, and the faces, names, and interpersonal dynamics of your new workplace. There may also be new software programs to adapt to; a change from tapes, used in class, to a digital dictation system; and formats and databases that go far beyond what you may have encountered in your medical transcription classroom.

A step-by-step evaluation of the working conditions and requirements of your new job, during the first few weeks, will help you develop optimal performance and job satisfaction. Even though every job is different, certain basic features are common to all medical transcription positions. These are discussed in this chapter.

THE WORKSTATION

A transcriptionist's workstation generally includes a desk and chair, a computer, a dictation system with headphones and a foot pedal, and storage cabinets or a hutch. The computer should have a processor equivalent to a 486 or faster Intel chip. Slower processors, such as a 386, will hamper production speed, requiring excessive waiting for screens to come up and reports to print. If the computer is an IBM-compatible machine, its operating system will almost certainly be either MS-DOS (which stands for Microsoft Disk Operating System) or Windows (either an older version, such as Windows 3.1, or any of the newer versions, such as Windows 95, 98, or 2000). Computers that run on MS-DOS may lack a mouse, a CD-ROM drive, and other "modern" features. Familiarizing yourself with multiple operating systems before completing school will reduce your training time and enhance your production once you are hired. Word processing programs in common use in transcription offices include Corel WordPerfect (version 5.1 or greater), Microsoft Word for Windows (version 6.0 or greater), and others. Some offices use Apple Macintosh computers, which run on their own operating system and run Macintosh-specific versions of programs such as WordPerfect and Microsoft Word.

The keyboard is one of the most essential components of the workstation. Test several for speed and ease of use, touch sensitivity, and how widely the keys are separated.

Ask if you can bring your own keyboard in to work, if so desired. Check the keyboard tray or holder for vertical tilt and horizontal movement, both for an ideal typing position and for variety to prevent repetitive-motion problems.

Headphones are another essential component of a transcriptionist's workstation. Several pair should be on hand, to prevent time lost if one is missing or damaged. Headphones should be light, comfortably padded, and adjustable and produce clear tones on each side.

The foot pedal should not require excess effort to depress. Changing the pedal at intervals from the left to right foot during the work-day will reduce repetitive motion and divide the stress between legs. Some transcriptionists elevate the foot pedal on a low platform for comfort.

A transcriptionist's desk should ideally be adjustable, or at least be at a height that is within a comfortable functioning range. The height should allow the transcriptionist to place the computer monitor near or at eye level and still have the keyboard low enough for relaxed typing. Drawers and an overhead storage bin should be provided.

The chair should be adjustable (both the seat height and the back support angle). It needs to have enough padding for an eight-hour day of sitting. It should roll on casters. The seat should swivel to allow access to the entire desktop without twisting the body.

Storage bins may be overhead, above the desk, with drawers below. Adequate storage will allow the transcriptionist to develop files and expand them over time. Proper lighting is also important; a combination of overhead lights and natural light from windows is preferred.

WORD PROCESSORS AND REPORT FORMATS

In addition to learning the nuances of different computer equipment and word processing software, the medical transcriptionist may need to learn various macros, or shortcut keys, that have been added to programs to speed productivity. Some dictators may request that you use predictated, "boilerplate" material, stored in macros, for repetitive reports (such as simple procedures like botulin toxin injections and complex yet consistent procedures such as cataract extractions). Material accessed by macros may or may not be fully credited to a transcriptionist's daily line count—find out.

A new transcriptionist will also encounter new formats, which he or she must learn and understand. Beyond the basic SOAP format of clinic notes (*s*ubjective, *o*bjective, *a*ssessment, *p*lan) and the standard formats for patient histories and physicals and discharge or operative summaries, the new transcriptionist may do specialty reports such as echocardiogram assessments, using elaborate preset templates (standardized forms), or complex radiology reports. Each employer may have subtle variations in report formats.

REFERENCE MATERIALS

Transcriptionists use medical dictionaries, formularies, and other references on a daily basis. Effective use of reference books and databases will improve accuracy and reduce "look-up time." Many transcriptionists build their own personal libraries over time, as well as using books provided by their employer.

Understanding how an individual reference book is organized *before* you need it promotes efficiency. This necessitates a brief advance study of each commonly used reference—its table of contents, text, index, and explanatory information. Is the reference divided by subject or alphabetically? Are there separate sections for brand-name and generic drugs? Does the reference provide hints, such as bulleted text, for which drugs to capitalize or not? Time invested in learning the style and nature of common references will be amply repaid. Even similar references may be organized differently and useful for different purposes. For example, some books are best for quickly looking up a drug name, whereas others are more cumbersome but include detailed dosage and pharmacological data. "Tabbing" reference books—for example, inserting tabs in a medical dictionary for diseases, syndromes, tests, and other entries frequently consulted—may help too. (Just be sure it's your own personal copy that you tab.)

In addition to texts, databases may also be available for consultation. These may include patient records, physician/provider lists, and lists compiled by in-house transcriptionists of unusual words, medical equipment, or medications. Access to Internet tools such as the National Library of Medicine Web site may also be available. Learning to "mine" databases for relevant information is worthwhile. Complete and accurate medical history numbers, addresses, and name spellings for each patient, taken from the database, are necessary to ensure proper delivery of transcribed reports. Words not found in standard references may also be located in this way.

WORK FLOW

Understanding the transcription procedures in a given organization promotes optimal output and job satisfaction; this section discusses the typical work input and output methods and formats found in most medical transcription offices.

Input

Most medical dictation is presented to the transcriptionist in one of two forms: on audiotapes or via a digital system that records dictation over telephone lines. If tapes are used, they must be transcribed tape by tape. A single tape may include dictation from one practitioner working in a single medical specialty or reports from multiple practitioners working in many specialties. Furthermore, they may vary in difficulty from straightforward family practice "chart notes" to complex operative or procedural reports.

Once reports are dictated, how does the work flow to the individual transcriptionist? Are tapes assigned by the supervisor or chosen freely by the transcriptionist? If freely selected, are they entirely optional, or are a certain number of "difficult" tapes or dictations required for each transcriptionist? Learning the current job process will allow individual management of work flow for improved performance.

For example, a new transcriptionist could select primarily chart notes in the first weeks, to practice and build confidence, with a small percentage of more challenging reports. Each week a higher percentage of challenging reports could be attempted. Also, transcriptionists often find they do some dictators better than others and some report types better than others. If allowed, emphasizing strong points while not neglecting challenges could produce a higher average line count. Transcription supervisors often are very skilled at helping the new transcriptionist manage the workload.

If a digital dictation system is employed, the "file server" computer will coordinate available reports and assign, or "queue" them, to individual transcriptionists. Here again, the amount of choice in how a transcriptionist manages his or her workload will vary among organizations but should be thoroughly understood. All transcription may be assigned by the supervisor or lead transcriptionist, or transcription may be assigned both by supervisors and by individual transcriptionists. Jobs may be "rejected" for specific reasons (such as insufficient time to complete a lengthy report before going home). The number of acceptable rejections per day or week must be known. The relative desirability of jobs will be learned over time—for example, surgeons tend to dictate quickly and generate more lines per minute than do other physicians; however, their dictation is often more challenging, requiring a higher level of skill to process quickly. Dictators known for frequent use of macro or boilerplate material are always very popular among transcriptionists. Conversely, non-native speakers with difficult accents, and dictators accustomed to jumping around or requiring frequent corrections, are less popular. The professional medical transcriptionist balances many different styles of dictation in a day's work, knowing that easy and difficult reports will equal out over time. However, strategic monitoring of the work flow, if permitted, may indicate the best time to take breaks or lunch in the hope of obtaining a desirable report on one's return.

Output

Work output is also of great concern to the medical transcriptionist. The immediate concern is for patient care providers to receive accurate and timely reports, to support continuity and excellence in the care they provide. This is the paramount service provided by medical transcriptionists. Also important, though, are the many copies and letters referred to health care providers outside the organization. These not only provide patients in outlying areas with records of services and procedures performed but also create an extended patient network, which may return additional business to the organization at a later date. Excellence in distributing letters and copies is therefore essential.

JOB DESCRIPTION

A newly hired transcriptionist should obtain a specific, detailed job description from his or her employer and review it to ensure it is clearly understood. Annual performance evaluations will be based on the criteria detailed in the job description. In particular, standards for productivity and accuracy must be met or exceeded over time. Therefore, keeping records of one's daily, weekly, and monthly productivity is advised to ensure compliance with organizational requirements. Having daily statistics on hand will prompt a transcriptionist to make up for a "slow day" as soon as possible. Similarly, regular quality reviews by supervisors offer both learning opportunities and the chance to correct deficiencies well before an annual review. Additional duties, such as proof-reading co-workers' reports for quality assurance and perhaps occasional phone duty, may also be assigned.

ON-THE-JOB PROFILE
Confidentiality

In World War II there were posters placed all over the United States that said "Loose lips sink ships." Secrecy was necessary to preserve national security. When I visited the New Jersey shore as a boy, our hotel still had "blackout curtains" to pull down before you turned on a light, in case enemy submarines were watching.

In medical transcription, confidentiality is an essential part of our service to patients. We are transcribing sensitive, often very personal reports. Our employers and our patients trust us to keep this information confidential. This discretion is often reinforced by the signing of a confidentiality statement on obtaining employment.

As you already know, a secret is not a secret when more than one person knows it. It's human nature to want to tell interesting things to others. That's why maintaining confidentiality is so important for the medical transcriptionist.

We hold the confidence of health care providers and patients because of our discretion. No matter what the nature of a report may be, it is not our business to repeat any portion of it to anyone. We earn the trust of others through our silence and our diligent work.

On rare occasions, we may transcribe a report in which the patient is a person well known to us. In this case, we may need to go beyond discretion to forgetfulness, and not recall that Cousin Ray has an incurable disease or friend Carl was injured in a motor vehicle accident.

Confidentiality is needed every day as a transcriptionist. Can you keep a secret?

SOCIAL ENVIRONMENT

Unlike working alone at home, working in an office with other transcriptionists provides a social environment, which can be both supportive and distracting. Having experienced transcriptionists on hand to help with difficult dictations is a significant benefit of working in an office setting. At the same time, however, extended personal conversations can detract from productivity. A careful balance needs to be maintained. A 5-minute conversation is a natural part of office life; a 15-minute conversation reduces hourly production by 25 percent! Maintaining positive, professional relations with coworkers contributes to overall office morale. Regular attendance at staff meetings also indicates a positive attitude and can provide insight into organizational needs and changes.

THE ELEMENTS OF PRODUCTION

Transcribing for an eight-hour shift is demanding and may take a period of adjustment for those unaccustomed to production-centered occupations. Even under optimal conditions—with a good chair, a glare-free computer monitor, and adequate lighting and ventilation—eight hours of sitting still and transcribing is hard work. Care should be taken to warm the hands gradually, building up speed over the first hour's transcribing rather than typing at top speed immediately. In cooler offices, sweaters or jackets should be kept on hand. Breaks for stretching or even brief walks will help maintain good circulation and thus good concentration. Pacing of reports is also important—transcribing less difficult reports, such as chart notes, at a higher speed will allow additional time for more challenging operative or procedure reports. Setting a time limit for researching individual words will prevent extended 10- or 15-minute searches, which inhibit productivity.

A combination of accuracy and high productivity is the daily goal of the medical transcriptionist. Maintaining quality while still producing rapid output is no easy task. Your first transcription job will be a learning experience. You will learn not only medical terminology, drug names, medical equipment, and report formats but also how to pace and structure your work to yield the best output. No one learns this overnight—learning it is a long process, requiring patience and persistence to attain a reasonable level of competence. Those who succeed in their first position, and subsequently develop a career, build a skill that anyone can be proud of. The experienced and competent medical transcriptionist remains a key player in the health care delivery team.

REVIEW QUESTIONS

1. What is boilerplate material? What is a macro?
2. On what basis might a job assigned to a transcriptionist be rejected?
3. How often do transcriptionists use medical reference books?
4. Are all drug reference books easily accessible?
5. Who determines how work flow proceeds in a transcription office?
6. Is a written job description necessary for a medical transcriptionist? Why or why not?

RELATED WEB SITES

MT DAILY NEW TRANSCRIPTIONISTS MESSAGE BOARD: http://www.mtdaily.com/mentors/newmts

MT DAILY NEW TRANSCRIPTIONISTS ARCHIVES: http://www.mtdaily.com/new.html

MEDICAL TRANSCRIPTION FORUM: "GETTING STARTED": America Online, keyword *medical transcriptionists*

NEW MEDICAL TRANSCRIPTIONISTS CONNECTION: http://grape.epix.net/~jphill/nmtc/

9
Career Development

LEARNING OBJECTIVES

- List three distinct types of career development
- Discuss the value of a personal reference library and filing system
- Explain the professional benefits of AAMT membership
- Describe several networking options for transcriptionists
- Discuss the increasing importance of Internet skills for the medical transcriptionist

 ON-THE-JOB PROFILE

Career Development

My transcribing career began in 1985. I was hired, through a temporary employment service, to transcribe for a small family practice clinic. My high-tech equipment was one of the first "electronic" typewriters. It had a small display that showed me part of the line I had just typed, before it printed it out. At the time, that was quite amazing.

Two years later I was working at a major clinic in Austin, Texas. This time I was back to an electric typewriter. We used carbon paper to create triplicate copies—and groaned every time a dictator asked us to back up several paragraphs and make a correction. That meant a lot of correcting fluid and paper handling. Changes in our basic document were always inconvenient, and the necessity of waiting for the carriage return after each line reduced our speed.

After my first year of employment, our supervisor wanted us to test something called a "word processor." I had been trained on a prototypical word processor (that had 60 separate function keys) back in 1984, and so I volunteered to lead the charge. I tried the new machine; found it much simpler, faster, and more functional than models past; and recommended it. The transition away from typewriters was not painless, though—one of our transcriptionists could not get the hang of word processing and was ultimately let go. It required a different mindset—words

ON-THE-JOB PROFILE   (continued)

were not immediately imprinted on paper, and text "wrapped" to the next line automatically without the typist's hitting the return key. Also, learning to proofread from a computer screen instead of a sheet of paper seemed odd at first, even to me.

In my next position, beginning in 1991 at a transcription service in Houston, I didn't handle any paper at all! All reports were printed out in a separate office and processed entirely by our clerks. We had to get it right on the screen or not at all! Wisely, this office employed two skilled proofreaders, called checkers, who double-checked our work before it went out to the Texas Medical Center. In five short years I had gone from handling carbons and triplicates to never touching a printed page.

In both of my subsequent transcription positions I typed up reports using word processing programs on Pentium computers, printing them out at remote sites (transcriptionists often get "bumped" from hospital office space and have to relocate to remote facilities when space gets tight). However, despite the emergence of several more sophisticated, graphically oriented word processing programs, both my previous and current employers still use WordPerfect 5.1, an older, DOS-based program. For transcription purposes, this is hard to argue with, as it has fewer visual distractions than the more graphic programs do and also allows very rapid access to macros.

Whatever the software used, transcription has changed almost as quickly as technology itself. With the gradual introduction of voice recognition software, expander programs such as Smartype, which suggest likely phrases while typing, and innovations not yet known, we can only expect the rate of change to accelerate and the future to belong to the flexible, the adaptable, and the technologically literate.

Becoming an experienced, professional medical transcriptionist is more than just learning high-speed typing and listening skills. Expanding your understanding of medical formats and language and interacting with professionals and transcription organizations can be the basis for a permanent and rewarding career. Career development encompasses, among other possibilities, three distinct areas: personal development, professional development, and technological development.

PERSONAL DEVELOPMENT

For a medical transcriptionist, personal development might include doing the following:

- Compiling a personal word list
- Developing a personal set of macros
- Compiling a personal collection of sample reports that show different standard formats

- Collecting a personal reference library
- Developing Internet skills
- Maintaining a personal set of files

The new transcriptionist inevitably encounters hundreds of unfamiliar terms beyond those learned in terminology courses. Starting and maintaining a personal list of unfamiliar terms builds a transcriptionist's medical vocabulary and helps avoid repeated inquiries for the same word. Word lists can be categorized, grouping names of medications, medical equipment, procedures, syndromes, and so forth. Although similar lists may already be available in the workplace, the process of writing a word down and committing it to memory is more effective for long-term retention. Capitalization of medication names may also be indicated, as well as usual dosages.

A word list should include a separate page for words with unusual spellings (such as HER-2/neu in oncology). Building a personal vocabulary notebook is an important part of the learning process, and your efforts in this regard will be repaid in reduced look-up time and an expanded knowledge base.

Similarly, macros, or word processing shortcuts, are an available feature of most word processing programs. Whatever word processing program you use probably comes with a number of preset macros, but building a collection of personal macros is likely to enhance your productivity. For example, certain common medical abbreviations (such as *WNL* for "within normal limits") may already be included as macros in your word processor, but others (such as *ITMT* for "in the meantime") may not be. The speech patterns of frequent dictators will suggest what phrases or passages to store in macros; certain speech dictators may use a number of "stock" sentences in every report. Thus, instead of having to type out "The patient was seen with Dr. _____, and the resident's H&P was reviewed. I personally examined and interviewed the patient," for each report, the transcriptionist can reduce the keystrokes to, for example, pressing the *Ctrl* key plus *R-E-S* for "resident," or *Ctrl* plus the dictator's surname. Macros can be either several letters (*Ctrl* plus *C-H-F* for "congestive heart failure," for example) or alphanumeric combinations (*T-1* for "the patient"; *T-1-r* for "The patient returns with"; *T-1-c* for "The patient complains of"; and so on). Maintain a consistent pattern for personal macros, as well as an organized list of all macros created. Macros improve production and also reduce the number of keystrokes to meet production quotas, thereby potentially reducing stress on the hands. Saving created macros on a separate disk will allow you to transfer them to other workstations or use them in subsequent jobs, and it will also protect against losing them.

Obtaining sample reports, either from your supervisor, an employee handbook, or more experienced transcriptionists, will also contribute to your personal development. Every transcription department will follow slightly different formats and styles for standard reports. Differences may be as simple as whether to insert two spaces or a paragraph return after the heading, before beginning the main text. More complex reports, such as operative reports or echocardiograms, may have their own preset formats, which also may vary by workplace. Also, style standards may vary between departments, even to the point where generally accepted abbreviations are altered to reduce keystrokes (for example, some departments may change *t.i.d.* and *b.i.d.* to *tid* and *bid*). Style and format standards are ultimately determined by each employer, although national format standards may be forthcoming. Becoming familiar with many different report types and formats is important, as is having the flexibility to meet an employer's needs, even if they conflict with stylistic conventions.

If policy permits, transcriptionists may keep copies of especially difficult reports or reports by particularly challenging dictators. Seeking out these reports and copying them is like taking out an insurance policy. Studying such reports may also expand your medical vocabulary. Research unusual words in your medical dictionary to be sure you know their meaning, not just their correct spelling. The ability to question and correct dictation requires a thorough understanding of medical terms.

Creating a personal reference library is another step in the personal development of a professional medical transcriptionist. Although reference books may be available in the office, owning your own copies allows greater interaction with them (such as underlining, writing notes in the margins, tabbing, and so on). It also provides the transcriptionist with a portable database that can be moved from office to home, or from job to job, as necessary. Ownership also allows the transcriptionist to obtain more specialized references not traditionally provided by employers. Any later transition to self-employment will be well supported by owning a collection of good reference books.

In addition, the Internet now provides a wealth of medical information that can be downloaded and placed in notebooks to supplement a personal library. Sites such as the MT Daily transcription Web site (http://www.mtdaily.com) offer current, detailed information and opportunities for interaction with other professionals. Subscribing to professional journals such as the *Journal of the American Association for Medical Transcription* and *Perspectives,* newsletters such as *The Latest Word,* and on-line journals such as *MT Monthly* can also provide a wealth of up-to-the-minute reference information.

Besides building a personal reference library, a new transcriptionist should also set up a personal file system from the first day of his or her employment. This will provide a place for initial hiring information, such as copies of contracts, benefit summaries, and employee handbooks. These documents can later be supplemented with timesheet records, quality assurance information, and all major employment-related data as it comes in. Keeping either a hanging file system or series of three-ring binders will provide an organized body of information. Complete files document a developing career and allow for easy reference when questions arise.

PROFESSIONAL DEVELOPMENT

Professional development for a medical transcriptionist might include the following:

- Networking locally
- Joining AAMT
- Enrolling in continuing education classes

- Becoming certified
- Engaging in relevant Internet-based activities
- Learning Joint Commission for Accreditation of Health Organizations (JCAHO) standards

Like charity, networking "begins at home"—by learning the names, faces, and background of classmates and then coworkers. The medical transcription field is full of interesting, intelligent, and experienced people whose hallmark is a desire to help others. Getting to know one's own associates well is the first step in developing a career network. Established transcriptionists will also know how to contact the local branch of AAMT, know transcriptionists at other institutions, and be familiar with the general style and nature of many different local health care facilities. Larger facilities may employ transcription services to handle overflow, and transcriptionists at such facilities can develop relationships with these professionals as well.

AAMT (the American Association for Medical Transcription) is a national organization for medical transcriptionists. Becoming a member of AAMT demonstrates a professional attitude toward one's career and also provides significant benefits. With its reference publications and certification process, AAMT sets the standard for excellence in medical transcription. Student memberships are also available, allowing interaction with professional transcriptionists while still completing one's education. Supporting AAMT strengthens the profession as a whole, through their publications, training, and advocacy for transcriptionists (such as their "Medical Transcriptionist's Bill of Rights," which is reproduced at the end of this chapter).

Continuing education, in addition to on-the-job learning, is a cornerstone of career development. In the medical field there are countless opportunities to expand one's knowledge and understanding. Continuing education can take the form of classes, seminars, or workshops on health-related topics; conferences, such as the AAMT annual meeting, where many educational sessions are included; review of professional journals, such as the *Journal of the American Association for Medical Transcription* and *Perspectives;* lectures or seminars provided by the employer in the workplace; or independent study of an organized nature to advance specific areas of interest. Continual advances in the health care field require ever more specialized knowledge from the medical transcriptionist and also provide opportunities for lifetime learning.

To become a Certified Medical Transcriptionist (CMT), a candidate must pass a two-part certification exam. Part I, the written portion, consists of multiple choice questions in such areas as medical terminology, anatomy and physiology, disease processes, English language, and professional development. Part II, the practical portion, consists of transcribing actual taped dictation from multiple specialties. Passing both portions of the exam earns the applicant the CMT designation. Continuing education requirements to maintain the certification promote continued learning and development. Certification also presents the transcriptionist as a serious professional and earns respect from health care colleagues.

The World Wide Web and Internet newsgroups provide additional avenues for professional development. Interacting with other medical transcriptionists via e-mail, Web sites (such as Keeping Abreast of Medical Transcription and MT Daily), and newsgroups lets transcriptionists connect with distant colleagues; exchange information and ideas; discuss new technologies, terminology, and business conditions; and keep up with trends. As the Web continues to expand, opportunities for professional growth and interaction will increase. Savvy medical transcriptionists will hone their Internet skills, incorporating this new technology into their professional lives and making the most of what is becoming a worldwide classroom.

The professional medical transcriptionist should also be aware of the standards necessary for institutional accreditation, as required by the Joint Commission for Accreditation of Healthcare Organizations (JCAHO). These may be found in JCAHO's comprehensive series of accreditation manuals for health care institutions; pay particular attention to the information management sections. These standards concern confidentiality of data and information, records protection, timeliness of data collection, records review for completeness, length of record retention, and many other requirements relevant to the practice of medical transcription.

For example, standard IM.7.1 states, "The hospital initiates and maintains a medical record for every individual assessed and treated." The transcription of these mandatory records is one of the bases for this profession.

Similarly, standard IM.7.3 states, "The medical record thoroughly documents operative or other procedures and the use of anesthesia."

Familiarity with JCAHO standards will help the new transcriptionist understand the legalities and regulations of the health care industry, as well as the importance of accurate and timely medical transcription.

 ON-THE-JOB PROFILE

Nonnative Speakers

Some years ago, a friend from Switzerland invited me and several other people over for dinner. English was not his primary language, and we all laughed when he served up "the spynitch" for a vegetable. He was not amused, however.

As anyone who has studied another language (note that I didn't say "foreign" language) knows, what you read in a textbook may not have much in common with the actual pronunciation. Persons learning English as a second language may learn to speak phonetically. Also, those speaking "the Queen's English" instead of American English may have considerably different pronunciations. As American cities grow more diverse and multicultural, medical transcriptionists will encounter an increasing number of nonnative speakers. This is one of the challenges—and interesting features—of our profession.

Learning to decipher various dialects, speech rhythms, pronunciations, and intonations can add much interest to our work. Remembering that words such as *nuchal* might be mispronounced "noochal," or *liver* might sound more like

ON-THE-JOB PROFILE   (continued)

"leever," can help facilitate accurate transcription. Sharing listening tasks with coworkers, if available, can help the new transcriptionist break in.

In addition to linguistic differences, difficulties in organization of dictation may require frequent backtracking. Lack of preparation time prior to dictation may necessitate long pauses while charts are reviewed. Both native and nonnative speakers can challenge the medical transcriptionist yet also present opportunities for an interesting and stimulating career.

TECHNOLOGICAL DEVELOPMENT

Technological development for the medical transcriptionist might include the following:

- Learning to use new word processing software
- Learning home computing applications
- Developing Internet searching skills
- Keeping up with advanced technologies

Medical transcriptionists should keep abreast of advances in word processing software, even if their employer is not planning to switch to a new program. Fluency in multiple word processing programs and versions will aid the employer if and when a new program is adopted, and it adds to the skill base a transcriptionist can bring to subsequent employers. Like most employers, transcription supervisors usually prefer "turnkey" employees—workers already versed in current programs, who do not require extensive training. The time and budget for extensive training is rarely available. Therefore, it is in every transcriptionist's own best interest to be familiar with several major word processing programs and to keep up with new developments as they occur. This need not require frequently purchasing software upgrades. Access to new programs may be obtained on a time-rental basis at copy shops. Relatively inexpensive seminars may be taken at computer training centers or community colleges, and these will possibly be reimbursed by the employer. ("Demo" versions of some software may also be downloaded from appropriate Web sites.)

Technological development should also include learning to use a modern home computer system, if at all possible. The benefits of home computer usage for transcriptionists—even those who work in an outside office—are numerous. This is because computer use at home is completely under the individual's control and is not confined to specific programs or databases, as it may be in the workplace. Study of a wide variety of programs may be undertaken at a relaxed pace. With an ISP the

Internet can be accessed from home, opening up vast storehouses of information. In addition, troubleshooting on a home computer may provide a better understanding of software and hardware, without the risk of damaging your employer's equipment.

Home computer systems tend to become obsolete fairly quickly. You can postpone this problem for as long as possible by purchasing a system with lots of RAM (random-access memory), a large hard drive, and the fastest processing chip available.

The evolution of voice-recognition software provides a good example of how system requirements tend to increase. Earlier, "discrete" (word-by-word) voice recognition programs required only 16 megabytes of RAM to operate, whereas later, more sophisticated continuous voice-recognition software needs at least 32 megabytes, and 64 or more megs is preferred. No matter how advanced a system is purchased, upgrading to newer technology in several years is probably inevitable. Much like continuing education, continuing skills development and periodic hardware upgrades will be a fact of life to maintain technological currency.

Internet searching skills for the transcriptionist are already desirable and will become a necessity in the future. Just as new versions of operating systems (such as Windows 2000) may come to incorporate Web browsers, transcription jobs may gradually come to incorporate e-mail, medical search engines, and full Internet access. In the near future, transcriptionists may routinely integrate multiple technologies (such as voice recognition, word processing, and word expansion software) and coordinate the flow of information rather than just enter it into a computer. In the next few years, sophisticated technologies—combined with good judgment, critical listening skills, and understanding—will help transcriptionists generate ever-higher volumes while still maintaining high quality.

The evolution of the medical transcriptionist's equipment from manual typewriters and carbon paper to electric typewriters, electronic typewriters, word processors, and finally enhanced word processors and voice-recognition software strongly suggests the likelihood of continued raising of the technological bar. Just as there will always be new terms and reports to learn, there will always be new tools with which to perform transcription. As these tools improve, the medical transcriptionist can take advantage of advances and refinements to increase production and improve cost-effectiveness, accuracy, and turnaround times.

REVIEW QUESTIONS

1. Name two valuable functions that macros serve.
2. Name at least one World Wide Web site that provides information on medical transcription.
3. List three professional development items.
4. List four technological development items.

RELATED WEB SITES

MT DESK GENERAL TRANSCRIPTION INFORMATION: http://www.mtdesk.com

MEDICAL TRANSCRIPTION SITES ON THE WORLD WIDE WEB: http://home.att.net/~protrans/index.htm and http://home.att.net/~protrans/medtrans.htm

LIST OF MEDICAL TRANSCRIPTION WEB RING SITES: http://www.webring.org/cgi~bin/webring?ring-mtring.list

10
Tricks of the Trade

LEARNING OBJECTIVES

- List several possible methods for improving your transcribing speed
- Discuss a logical search strategy for unfamiliar medical terms
- Develop at least five production enhancement tips
- List five components of critical listening

ON-THE-JOB PROFILE
Real-World Transcription

After 14 years of transcribing for clinics, transcription services, and hospitals, my goals are fairly simple:

1. I want to meet or exceed my required line count every day.
2. I want to maintain the highest possible accuracy.
3. I want to work as efficiently as possible, so I still have time to take my lunch and breaks while meeting my employer's standards.

What does it take to do this? Let's look at a typical day. I usually type 20 to 25 reports of varying lengths in a seven-hour shift. My job requires a minimum production of 115 to 130 lines per hour. After breaks and nonproductive time are counted, I need to crank out about 750 lines per shift to meet the standard.

There are many faster transcriptionists than I in our office. Plus, my 45-year-old hands take about an hour to warm up. However, I try to use my time effectively for maximum results. I say good morning to my coworkers but avoid lengthy conversations, which cut into productive time. If my first two or three reports are fairly long (five minutes of dictation or longer), I relax and enjoy the ride. However, if they are short (three minutes or less), I work more rapidly to get them out of the way, in the hope that longer reports will follow.

ON-THE-JOB PROFILE (continued)

In an hour I can generate about 130–140 lines for longer reports but only around 100 lines for short reports requiring multiple headings or copies. Extended reports such as psychological evaluations, which can often involve 20–30 minutes of dictation, may generate well over 150 lines per hour. I have to admit I sometimes take advantage of these "bonus lines" to have an easier day.

I make extensive use of the personal macros I have built up over three years in my current position. Certain specialties, such as cardiology, lend themselves to macro use particularly well. For example, "The patient has a history of congestive heart failure, coronary artery bypass grafting, and myocardial infarction" can be typed using macros as follows: *T1* ("The patient") *Hx* ("has a history of") *CHF* ("congestive heart failure") *CABG* ("coronary artery bypass grafting") *MI* ("myocardial infarction"). Using alphanumeric macros also allows me to cover variations of standard phrasing:

> *T1*—"The patient"
> *T1c*—"The patient complains of"
> *T1d*—"The patient denies any"
> *T1s*—"The patient states that"
> and so on.

Years of listening to dictation has attuned me to the consistent phrasing used by many physicians in their reports, yielding macros such as these:

> *pleas*—"We had the pleasure of seeing your patient . . ."
> *tol*—"The patient tolerated the procedure well and was returned to the recovery room in satisfactory condition."
> *ret*—"The patient returns to clinic today with a complaint of . . ."
> *sup*—"The patient was taken to the operating room and placed in the supine position."

Even if a macro yields more text than is needed for a particular report, it's often easier to delete the excess than to type the whole thing from scratch. While working, I keep track of the lines in each report. I know that after three hours of work I should have generated about four hundred lines. I also build in a margin of error to ensure good daily productivity.

In transcribing, human error is inevitably a factor. After four or five hours of fast typing, I start to tire. After lunch, I may feel sleepy and my output may decline. The sedentary nature of transcription can sometimes lead to daydreaming. That makes taking breaks and short, brisk walks mandatory to keep alert!

Some of the pressures of this business include "stat" dictations and rapid turnaround times. High volumes, in conjunction with inadequate staffing, are another source of stress for transcriptionists. We are not immune to budget cutbacks; employees who resign may not be replaced, making it difficult for those who

To the new medical transcriptionist, the requirements of the first transcribing position may seem daunting. Averaging well over one hundred lines per hour while having to look up countless new terms, remember unfamiliar formats and physician names, and develop an exceptional standard of accuracy is not easy. Bringing up your typing speed from 60–70 words per minute to near or above 100 words per minute also presents a significant challenge, as does learning to proofread rapidly and expertly on a computer monitor.

What tips might an experienced transcriptionist offer a new colleague? What tricks and techniques do experienced transcriptionists use to work their "verbal magic" on a daily basis?

TYPING SPEED

Many factors and variables contribute to an excellent typing speed. Natural ability or talent is only one of those factors. Since all individuals have different ability levels, experimentation and practice are required to determine the fastest, most accurate method for any given individual. Variables that can be adjusted include the familiar speed drills and the practice gained from transcribing eight hours a day. On a practical level, varying the height and angle of the keyboard for best results, changing to a different keyboard or different style of keyboard, practicing words that are difficult to type quickly, practicing rapid retrieval of macros and integrating macro use into one's typing style, typing while looking at one's monitor or hands or even with one's eyes closed to enhance one's sense of touch, and practicing gradual increases in speed to the highest reasonably accurate level are all worth trying. Experimentation may provide the best individual results.

Typing speed is only one factor in overall transcribing speed and productivity. Finding the highest possible speed at which smooth, consistent production can occur is worth a certain amount of trial and error. Varying your typing speed during the course of a shift is also important, as is having several working speeds to choose from—both relaxed and intense—as the work flow and circumstances dictate.

PATIENT DATA

Entering patient data in report headings can consume a significant amount of a transcriptionist's time. This is particularly true if all information is not consolidated in a single, easily accessible database. Becoming familiar with the spelling of physicians' names and their specialties, which will happen gradually, may be accelerated by a weekly review of names, as well as jotting down unusual spellings in your notebook. Similarly, a transcriptionist needs to remember external providers to whom copies are regularly sent. In the transcription office, local, regional, and even national physician directories, or on-line directories, may be provided to allow correct addressing. Learning how these directories are organized will reduce look-up time. A national Zip Code directory is also a useful tool.

LOOK-UP TIME

Another factor affecting productivity is the time needed to look up unfamiliar medical terms and other information. Developing effective search strategies can reduce this time to a minimum. This will involve identifying the basic category of the word in question—is it a medication? an anatomical term? a piece of medical hardware? a surgical term?—and then following a logical path through the appropriate reference book, such as a medical dictionary, a surgical reference book, or a more general reference such as *Current Medical Transcription* by Vera Pyle.

For example, suppose you hear a word on a dictation tape that sounds like "inelpril" and is used in the context of a list of medications. You could search for the correct spelling of this term by "running the vowels" in a drug reference, looking for *analpril, enelpril, inelpril, onelpril,* and *unelpril,* until you encounter a real drug name (in this case, *enalapril*). Obvious surgical terms, such as suture types, can be checked under the most relevant heading (*suture,* in this case) as well as the given name (*Ethilon suture*) in a surgical dictionary or a relevant specialty dictionary (such as orthopedics).

Cross-referencing is another technique for word hunting. For a syndrome, for example, look under the specific syndrome name (*acquired immune deficiency syndrome,* for instance) as well as under the word *syndrome.* Also, check possible variant spellings under both listings. If the word you are after is not found under *syndrome,* look under *disease.* Keep good basic medical reference books on your desk for convenience.

PRODUCTION TIPS

As with most people employed in production-based activities, experienced transcriptionists develop coping skills to improve their productivity while maintaining comfort and an enjoyable workplace. These tips may include the following:

1. Starting work 5 or 10 minutes early each day to "stay ahead of the game" psychologically, thereby feeling more relaxed instead of pressured.
2. Bringing a lunch to save travel time to and from restaurants.
3. Typing one or two longer reports at top accurate speed to build line count.
4. Keeping a file of difficult reports for future reference.

5. Designing specific macros for repetitive paragraphs commonly used by individual dictators.

6. Designing macros (if not already available) for repetitive procedure reports.

7. Designing subheading macros that follow standard formats, such as for physical examinations.

8. Working 5 or 10 minutes past quitting time occasionally, if necessary, to complete a final report, rather than finishing 10 minutes early with an inadequate line count.

MADE IN JAPAN

Hazel Tank

What does it mean, this "quality assurance" that we have all been hearing so much about these past few years? How come, all of a sudden, we are hearing all about TQM (Total Quality Management), TQL (Total Quality Leadership), CIP (Continuous Improvement Process), and the like? Let's review the history books a bit.

During World War II, Professor W. Edwards Deming was concerned that because U.S. industrial production was at such a furious peak, the resultant quality of American manufactured goods would suffer. He approached various corporations with his ideas of improving quality. As was to be expected, they laughed him out of their offices.

After World War II, Dr. Deming went to Japan. He set about teaching Japanese managers and workers how to work better and faster. The Japanese listened. Over the next few years, American corporations watched their sales go down as more and better Japanese goods flooded the market. Working Americans were quick to catch the drift of what was happening and turned in droves to Japan and Germany for high-quality goods.

Medical transcription is a service, and services need to be of the highest quality possible to be in demand. A service company or transcription department is the sum of its individuals. Should we as individuals not seek and meet high quality standards, our clients/employers will turn to someone who does. Meeting quality standards does not mean simply getting the demographics or a report correct; it involves using correct medical terminology, English, and grammar; sticking to prescribed formats; and ensuring readability of the document created. Improve the quality, and the quantity will improve as well. It's been proven time and again.

PROOFREADING TIPS

There are several components to proofreading medical transcription in a real-world office setting. All of these are based on a good working knowledge of English grammar and spelling. During actual transcribing, mistakes may be corrected "on the fly," or while typing, as much as possible. When the report draft is completed, the transcriptionist then carefully proofs the entire document, making further necessary corrections. The third and final step is running and monitoring the word processor's spell checker. While proof-reading, the transcriptionist should pay particular attention to mistakes that will *not* be caught by the spell checker, such as homophones and words that are not misspelled but are used incorrectly or in the wrong context. In addition to ensuring correct spelling and grammar, a transcriptionist must be sure to correctly capture the dictator's meaning. Understanding the difference in meaning between similar-sounding words, such as *perineal* versus *peroneal,* is also part of the transcriptionist's job.

CRITICAL LISTENING SKILLS

Health care providers dictate reports in many different settings, often with significant background noise. Not all dictators have English as their native language. Adjusting to accents is ever more necessary for transcriptionists in multicultural urban areas. Not only pronunciation but also phrasing and inflection may vary considerably between native and nonnative speakers of English. Also, even some native speakers have unusual speech patterns, and all dictators speak in different speeds and tones. Developing a critical ear is essential for successful transcription. Borrowing techniques from more experienced transcriptionists can facilitate this development.

Tips for more critical listening could include the following:

1. Listen to exactly what the dictator says, rather than trying to anticipate what is going to be said.
2. Focus on the spoken word rather than on distracting background noises.
3. Identify the initial letter of an unclear word, then test other, similar-sounding letters (such as *b, d,* and *p*) until a match is found.
4. For a difficult passage, listen again, without typing, to reduce noise congestion.
5. Vary the volume and speed controls.
6. Leave a blank space for a difficult passage, finish the rest of the report, and then return with a "fresh ear" (or borrow a coworker's ear).

A careful balance between production and quality-control goals will generate the best output. The challenge for both new and experienced transcriptionists is to meet high standards of productivity and accuracy on a daily basis. Developing individual techniques for achieving optimal results, in addition to those mentioned in this chapter, will create a broader base of skills from which to draw. Learning from colleagues, and sharing one's own techniques, will benefit the entire transcription department.

REVIEW QUESTIONS

1. What is the best technique for locating unfamiliar words in a medical reference book?
2. What does "correcting on the fly" mean?

3. How can familiarity with physicians' names be expedited?

4. What are the three steps of high-quality proofreading?

5. Name three tips for better critical listening.

RELATED WEB SITES

TAPDANCE MEDICAL TRANSCRIPTION SKILLS TESTING: http://www.priassoc.com/taptrans.htm

WINNING STRATEGIES FOR HOME-BASED MEDICAL BUSINESSES: http://www.luresa.com

MT MONTHLY JOURNAL: http://www.mtmonthly.com

ERGONOMIC ACCESSORIES: http://www.safecomputing.com/index.htm

11
Occupational Hazards and Benefits

LEARNING OBJECTIVES

- Discuss several job-related problems common to medical transcription
- List several hazards of a sedentary occupation
- Explain the cause and nature of carpal tunnel syndrome
- Describe the three ways in which transcriptionists may be paid
- State the variety of working hours that may be available in medical transcription departments

 ON-THE-JOB PROFILE
Occupational Hazards

Like any job, medical transcription has its occupational hazards as well as its joys and benefits. Some risks are obvious and straightforward; others "come with the territory" but aren't always what you might expect.

In the dozen or so years that I've been wearing headphones to transcribe, I think my hearing has slowly deteriorated. This may simply be an effect of my advancing age and my male gender, but I suspect it's also related to having that voice so close to my ears for hours a day. Nowadays, I have trouble differentiating voices in crowded restaurants or hearing my wife when she speaks to me from the next room. Occupational condition? Possibly. I can certainly say a corollary is that, after eight hours of listening, I want it fairly quiet when I come home. I used to listen to music often but now rarely do. After a long shift, I feel like my ears are all used up!

There are many other similarly subtle changes that I relate to being a medical transcriptionist. I've heard so many unfortunate medical stories in dictations that I'm less sympathetic to minor complaints than I used to be. No matter what someone tells me, I've probably typed worse within the past week. And there's a certain frustration about listening to problems but not being able to directly

ON-THE-JOB PROFILE   (continued)

provide the care. Sometimes I wish I could just drive over to the emergency room and help out, had I the necessary skills.

There's been a lot of publicity about carpal tunnel syndrome for typists, and I have seen this on the job from time to time. I'm always saddened when I see a transcriptionist wearing a splint but still typing away at high speed, financially unable to take the extended time off to fully recover. One day the lead transcriptionist where I worked in Austin, Texas, a young woman of about 27, called in sick because she woke up and had no feeling in one of her arms! She had been working overtime, typing more than 60 hours per week, and it caught up with her. But she was back the next day, apparently much improved, and still continues in transcription, 10 years later.

Every job also has interpersonal hazards, and these can vary from small to life-threatening. One day at the clinic in Austin I heard shots ring out in our parking lot. I soon learned that an angry ex-husband had gunned down one of our nurses, his ex-wife, with whom he had been engaged in a prolonged custody battle. Similarly, while working at a hospital in Seattle, I heard reports that two female transcriptionists on the evening shift had gotten into an actual fistfight! All human beings, whatever they do for a living, are delicate and potentially dangerous creatures.

Perhaps the greatest problem associated with a transcription career is financial. The amount of skill required to do this work is not generally recognized or appreciated, and as a result the compensation may be more modest than it should be. This is beginning to change, as programs such as incentive pay and straight production pay allow better earnings. Aside from National Transcription Week, though, I think transcriptionists as a whole are taken for granted. I've heard of many nursing strikes, but never a strike by transcriptionists. We work very hard, but the secondary, "in the background" nature of our work in medicine seems to limit our status—and our pay—to some extent. However, as computers and the Internet become more fully integrated into health care, I believe that the emerging role of the medical transcriptionist as a medical information coordinator will improve our status. The increasing complexity of medicine, and the opportunity to quickly include data from the Internet into patients' charts, will increase opportunities for the medical transcriptionists of the future.

The occupation of medical transcription has its own specific challenges and difficulties, as well as its own unique rewards. Understanding these risks and benefits can not only promote a balanced picture of the profession but also help prevent potential problems encountered over the course of a career.

There are several distinct job-related problems common to medical transcription. These include relative social isolation, organizational isolation, health problems (such as undue weight gain) from a sedentary lifestyle, upper-body discomforts from extended typing, and carpal tunnel syndrome.

The reaction to social isolation arising from fairly constant headphone use varies among individuals. Gregarious people, fond of frequent verbal interactions on the job, may feel constrained by the limiting nature of headphones. Similarly, people who enjoy listening to music while working may be frustrated by its absence. Even when proofreading or resting without headphones on, transcriptionists are aware of the clock ticking and productivity demands, and thus may be reluctant to engage in extended socializing. On a long-term basis, this narrowed focus may be undesirable for extroverted, highly social people.

A comparable, and more economically significant, problem is the transcriptionist's relative isolation within the health care organization. A busy transcriptionist does not attend meetings, engage in office politics, or interact much with coworkers; rather, he or she creates reports and processes information. This can mean feeling "out of the loop" in regard to organizational changes and opportunities. Particularly when backlogs are high and the work is piled up, transcriptionists have little time for the necessary social activities often required for organizational advancement. Although opportunities for promotion certainly exist for transcriptionists, the time and energy to take advantage of them may not be available.

Transcriptionists' low visibility may be associated with their lower wages and status, compared to that of frontline workers such as nurses and therapists. Despite the vital function transcriptionists perform, their location—often well away from "control centers" such as nursing stations, sometimes even in external offices—may reduce their visibility and hence the recognition of their worth.

ON-THE-JOB PROFILE
Making Sense

It's easy to get into a "zone" while transcribing—have a great typing speed, cut through all stray background noise, transcribe exactly what the dictator said—and still not be doing your job. That's because our task is not only to transcribe what has been dictated but also to verify that it all makes sense.

This can be as simple as noticing that a physician gives "January 4, 1962," as the date of birth for an "87-year-old patient." A common example of a continuity problem would be the dictation of "left arm" for several paragraphs, then "right arm" for the rest of the same procedure. Another frequent inconsistency is switching between "male" and "female" to describe a patient who has not undergone a gender-change operation. Checking names may give the answer, but not always.

Similarly, transcribing medication dosages requires care and familiarity. A dose of 10 mg in one paragraph and 100 mg in a later paragraph is certainly possible—if a care provider has specifically altered that dose. Also, many medications are routinely prescribed at certain dosages, such as 40 mg of Lasix—so a dose of 400 mg of Lasix, although possible, might very well be an error.

ON-THE-JOB PROFILE (continued)

It is not our task to change an unfamiliar dosage, merely to question obvious inconsistencies, check drug reference books, and even contact the dictator if necessary to verify accuracy. And since medications can be given in micrograms, milligrams, and even grams, we need to be certain that inconsistent text is corrected.

When transcribing operative reports, we must not only listen carefully but also trace a mental image of the procedure in our minds. If a Bankart shoulder procedure is under way, the anterior cruciate ligament in the knee probably won't be referred to. If cataract surgery is in progress, the metatarsals or metacarpals probably will not be involved. Of help to transcriptionists is knowing the difference between words with similar sounds, such as *perineal* and *peroneal.*

It all boils down to understanding, which evolves over time and from familiarity with hundreds, even thousands of varied reports. It also takes concentration, focusing on the report at hand, and dedication to wanting to make each report as accurate as humanly possible. Even now, after 14 years of transcribing, I get excited to think that each report I type helps contribute to improving someone's health, and each inconsistency I correctly question raises the quality of the medical record.

The sedentary lifestyle of transcribing can present certain health hazards. Undesired weight gain, deconditioning, and more serious long-term health problems may develop if full-time transcribing is not offset by regular aerobic activity. Additionally, the fatigue resulting from eight or more hours of rigorous mental activity may make the prospect of physical exercise after work unattractive. Keeping fit throughout one's career may be more difficult for transcriptionists than it is for physically active workers.

Certain physical discomforts in the neck, shoulders, and back may be related to regular transcribing. The process of holding the arms extended for hours while typing places stress on the upper body musculature. Also, many transcriptionists work more than 40 hours per week, "moonlighting" in addition to their regular positions. This places further stress on their bodies and reduces the time and energy available for exercise.

New technologies may lead to new health problems. Persons changing to voice recognition software, for example, may place strain on their voices. Such stresses should be factored in to achieve a complete picture of the occupational risks to transcriptionists.

Perhaps the most recognized of repetitive-motion injuries related to transcribing is carpal tunnel syndrome. The median nerve and flexor tendons run through an opening between the wrist bones and the transverse carpal ligament. Irritation of the tendons and resulting thickening can increase pressure in the carpal tunnel, squeezing the median nerve. Impaired nerve function can cause numbness and pain in the hand.

A medical transcriptionist who averages 150 lines of 65 characters per hour performs 9,750 keystrokes per hour, or approximately 75,000 keystrokes each eight-hour day. Over a period of years, this places significant stress on the body and may lead to difficulties such as carpal tunnel syndrome. Increased production requirements, to promote cost-effectiveness and rapid turnaround times; faster equipment, such as word processors versus electric typewriters; and moonlighting or overtime work to enhance individual income may further contribute to repetitive motion injuries among medical transcriptionists.

On the positive side, the occupational advantages specific to medical transcription are also numerous and significant. These include the potential for good to excellent pay and benefits, flexibility in working hours, the possibility of self-employment and working at home, interesting work, the status associated with being a health care professional, and a uniquely focused and personally-rewarding occupation.

Although wages vary from state to state as well as within metropolitan areas, transcriptionists on the whole have many opportunities to earn a respectable income. Transcriptionists are paid not only hourly but sometimes hourly with "incentive pay" or on a straight production basis. Those who opt for self-employment may set their own rates, based on community standards and supply and demand. In busy metropolitan areas, opportunities for moonlighting and for overtime may routinely exist or be easily created. Those able to work extra hours or on a production pay basis may substantially bolster their incomes. The chance to be paid for extra effort, rather than merely for time put in, adds to the potential financial benefits of medical transcription. In this profession, working harder is often rewarded. Also, the necessity of providing accurate medical records for a growing and aging population suggests there will be no shortage of work in the years ahead.

In addition to salary considerations, job benefits are considerable advantages for those medical transcriptionists working as employees. The value of adequate health and dental insurance rises each year, as does the value of sick days, annual leave, and personal holidays. Pension and 401K plans, if available, offer long-term advantages for permanent employees. However, the trend among many employers is to reduce employee benefits or increase payroll deductions for benefits, increasing their cost to employees. Therefore, if a job provides full benefits, it will become ever more valuable. Finding employers who offer "full coverage" is of great advantage to the medical transcriptionist.

The possibility of flexible working hours, although not universal for transcriptionists, is nonetheless a substantial advantage for those who obtain them. Larger health care employers often have evening as well as day shifts, and some provide 24-hour service. To manage the work flow and maintain employee satisfaction, work hours may be adjusted based on individual scheduling needs and the availability of desk space, rather than conforming to a rigid 8:00 to 5:00 workday. Weekend coverage may also be required, and working on the weekend could free up one or two weekdays for personal business. Having choices in work hours may be very helpful for parents with child care responsibilities. Being able to tailor one's own schedule, if allowed, lends a sense of independence to the medical transcriptionist. Conversely, being willing to work extra hours or weekend rotations is only fair, to help out the employer as the workload fluctuates.

The possibility of self-employment for medical transcriptionists adds a further dimension to this field. Home computer ownership at the Pentium level places the independent transcriptionist on a par with the office worker, in terms of word processing ability. Those who choose to work for themselves and have the experience and ability to do so successfully may have more control of their working hours and, to some extent, their income. This option, when appropriate, expands the lifestyle choices of the medical transcriptionist.

The chance to perform interesting work, although it is for some a less immediate concern than attractive wages and benefits, is a definite long-term advantage of a career in medical transcription. The variety of medical conditions, situations, and personal concerns encountered by a transcriptionist seems endless. The opportunity to learn new terms on a daily basis is priceless. Knowledge gained from transcribing is continuing education at its best. Combining that knowledge with the development of Internet-based research skills and skills in computer operating systems and programs contributes to a high level of employability as well as personal development and satisfaction.

The status associated with the medical field is another intangible yet important asset for the medical transcriptionist. Just as physicians and nurses are held in the highest regard in our society, those who support them in a skilled and professional manner earn respect for their knowledge and labor. Nor is this status easily gained, for the working transcriptionist struggles every day to keep up with new developments, terms, and techniques.

Finally, the medical transcriptionist has a uniquely focused occupation, derived from the particular concentration required to transcribe complex dictations quickly and accurately. When transcribing an operative report, for example, the transcriptionist mentally follows the surgeon from the initial incision to the wound closure and return to the recovery room, listening not only for correct wording but also for the logic and meaning of every sentence, to detect inaccuracies. This process takes place while typing rapidly and screening out stray noises on and off the dictation system. Those who appreciate pure and undiluted work can derive great enjoyment from the process of medical transcription. The combination of financial, personal, and educational rewards creates a very attractive and challenging profession.

REVIEW QUESTIONS

1. How can organizational isolation affect medical transcriptionists?
2. What are the two major symptoms of carpal tunnel syndrome?
3. Are transcriptionists ever paid on a production basis?
4. Is weekend coverage ever required for hospital-transcription offices?

RELATED WEB SITES

CARPAL TUNNEL SYNDROME PAGE: http://www.netaxs.com/~iris/cts/welcome.htm

ERGONOMIC LINKS: http://www.etcnewyork.com/ergli.html

TYPING INJURY FREQUENTLY ASKED QUESTIONS: http://www.tifaq.com

REPETITIVE STRESS INJURY NETWORK NEWSLETTER: http://www.tifaq.com/rsinet/index.html

12
Opportunities for Advancement

LEARNING OBJECTIVES

- List several employment opportunities above the transcriptionist level
- Define the functions and role of the lead transcriptionist
- Explain the duties of the quality assessment specialist
- Explain the duties of the transcription supervisor
- Describe the background and duties of a transcription instructor

ON-THE-JOB PROFILE
Production 101

Although I've been a medical transcriptionist for 14 years, it was certainly not my first production-based job. That came much earlier, in the summer after my junior year of college. I made a rather drastic transition from studying English literature at the University of Texas to working full-time for a restaurant supply company. This "food factory" supplied a variety of prefab foods for a very nice nine-restaurant chain.

I went from reading Chaucer and James Joyce to being "the meatball man." On Mondays another young man and I would grind up eight hundred pounds of beef in a meat grinder. This involved lifting 80-pound boxes of meat and dumping them into a large hopper. After the meat was ground it ran through the meatball machine, which popped out little red balls that slid down a belt onto waiting trays. On Tuesdays I would set up a large kettle and boil the meatballs one tray at a time. The cooked meatballs were then set aside in a large plastic "bathtub" in the cooler. Then, on Wednesday morning, the crew and I would make eight hundred gallons of barbecue sauce in a seven-foot vat. This entailed dumping a 25-pound sack of salt, 100-pound sacks of flour, and 450 one-gallon cans of ketchup into the vat. I have no idea why larger drums of ketchup were not available, but we had to individually open 450 cans and carefully scrape out the contents

ON-THE-JOB PROFILE   (continued)

so nothing was wasted. Thursdays were devoted to placing the meatballs in the barbecue sauce and sealing them in one-gallon paper cartons. Fridays were wonderful, for then I was exposed to the many other products we produced.

For example, we would process three hundred frozen ducks each week. One of the butchers would cut each duck in half with a power saw, and I would catch it after it had been halved. The ducks were subsequently cooked, deboned, and bagged. A skilled and diligent worker in this factory could choose from a variety of wonderful tasks to perform. Slackers, however, received the ultimate punishment—the "cheese line." This line processed a "homemade" cheese spread that was poured into eight-ounce cups. At the front end of the line, workers stacked six cups of cheese, pushed them forward onto a belt, and then stacked six more. All day, like robots—one, two, three, four, five, six, shove. And the front of the line was the good end.

At the back of the line, one worker caught sealed boxes of cheese spread, ran over to a wooden pallet, stacked them, and ran back for more. Grab two, run, drop two, run, all day long. We made a lot of cheese spread, which was sold in stores as well as our restaurants. Eight hours on the cheese line was enough to ruin anyone's day.

Although medical transcription is a far cry from working in a food factory, the stresses and repetitions of production are similar. However, medical transcription also offers opportunities for advancement above and beyond the production worker's level. Even the new transcriptionist can keep an eye out for unexpected chances to move UP.

After three to five years of progressively more challenging work, rising from the clinic level to multispecialty, a medical transcriptionist may want to look for advancement opportunities. These can include becoming a lead transcriptionist, a quality assessment specialist, a transcription office supervisor, a private service supervisor, a transcription instructor, or a medical information specialist. Although it must be emphasized that significant transcribing experience must precede moving into any of these positions, there are nonetheless many opportunities to expand beyond basic medical transcription.

The lead transcriptionist "anchors" a transcription shift, providing support to the transcription staff. He or she must not only possess exceptional transcription ability but also be thoroughly trained in the organization's computer system—beyond its word processing program—so as to be able to troubleshoot employee problems. His or her training may also extend to the dictation equipment used, as well as organizational policies and procedures. The lead is generally given much more "nonproductive time" than a regular transcriptionist, in order to attend to a variety of duties and maintain a steady work flow from the group. The lead may also be involved in quality assurance, maintaining production records for employees, and researching new or difficult terms. The lead acts as a bridge between staff and management, maintaining active communications and transferring necessary information to the other transcriptionists.

The quality assessment (QA) specialist often works in a larger office or transcription service, supervising the accuracy of the work produced. Excellent editing and proofreading skills are required, as well as the ability to consistently scrutinize reports over extended periods of time. A superior knowledge of medical and anatomical terminology, as well as expert medical reference skills, enables the QA specialist to detect inaccuracies and inconsistencies, research unusual terms, and refine large numbers of transcribed reports for the highest possible level of accuracy. Conveying terminology updates and continuing education opportunities to staff may also be included in the job description.

The transcription supervisor manages all operations of a transcription department, performing managerial functions such as budgeting, staffing, dealing with vendors and technicians, timekeeping, delegating, system planning and troubleshooting, and reporting to the medical records department and health care providers as appropriate. The supervisor may also monitor staff production and accuracy, the type of work assigned to different transcriptionists, personal staff concerns, and the overall output and quality of the department. This demanding position requires a combination of technical, supervisory, and interpersonal skills, in addition to a thorough knowledge of medical transcription practices and procedures. In addition to maintaining departmental performance, transcription supervisors must plan for and adapt to changing technologies and fluctuations in the workload. Upgrading computers and computer software, managing computer networks, and testing new expander and voice-recognition software are all tasks that the transcription supervisor may either perform or delegate.

A self-employed transcriptionist whose workload expands beyond his or her capacity to keep up may evolve into a private service supervisor. To fulfill contractual obligations or accept additional opportunities, such a transcriptionist might hire subcontractors. Over time he or she might become a regular employer, and consequently a supervisor. Expanding workloads may require anywhere from several to more than a dozen subcontractors. Making the move to private service supervisor means performing several new functions, including obtaining and maintaining accounts and records, assisting subcontractors with difficult dictation, maintaining quality control, and supervising the transfer of information from subcontractors to clients. As a result, the new supervisor may perform reduced or minimal transcription himself or herself. The private supervisor works without the benefit of an established transcription office and its management team, taking on many different jobs simultaneously. However, despite the long hours and complex work, a private supervisor has the opportunity to be paid from the labor of others as well as his or her own personal effort and thus is not limited to a fixed hourly or production-based salary.

A transcription instructor may teach in a vocational or community college, conducting day or evening classes to accommodate adult students' work schedules. Instruction may include basic transcribing skills, guiding students through graduated dictations, and also teaching related courses such as medical terminology, anatomy and physiology, basic pharmacology, or even medical ethics. Unlike transcription itself, which generally requires only a high school diploma and a transcription course to begin, teaching in a community college setting may require a bachelor's or even a master's degree. In addition to transcription experience, the instructor should possess prior teaching experience, excellent proofreading abilities, and strong interpersonal skills.

An instructor's pay may be based on "contact hours," or classroom time, but time spent in traveling to the work site, class preparation, and grading should be taken into consideration. Thus, an impressive wage of $30 per contact hour might actually amount to $15 per work hour after grading and class preparation are factored in. Teaching experience may lead to additional opportunities such as seminars, guest lectures, and technical writing, however.

A medical information specialist builds on the skills obtained through transcribing, combining his or her knowledge of medical terminology with library research and Internet searching skills to obtain current medical information for diverse clients, ranging from individuals to health care professionals or hospitals. A home computer with Internet access can provide extensive data on many medical topics. This on-line information can be supplemented with trips to the nearest medical or university library, as indicated.

For individual clients, the combination of general health information with more technical medical articles may be most helpful. Institutions lacking medical libraries or staff development departments might also be receptive to hiring an "on-call" medical information service. Beginning this business as a sideline, after hours, allows for gradual development without compromising household income.

As medical transcription and computer science become ever more closely related, transcriptionists may find their knowledge of word processors, operating systems, Internet searching, voice recognition software, and general research ever more in demand. By expanding the focus of the profession, opportunities can be developed, both in home and office settings, to fulfill a greater role in the delivery of health care and the dissemination of vital medical information. For the entrepreneurially minded medical transcriptionist, advances in technology and changes in health care delivery offer significant possibilities for increased income.

REVIEW QUESTIONS

1. Why does the lead transcriptionist have more nonproductive time than a regular transcriptionist?

2. Which employee in a transcription office plans for and adapts to changes in workloads?

3. At what level does a medical transcription instructor generally teach?

4. What are the functions of a medical information specialist?

RELATED WEB SITES

CLERICAL SUPERVISOR: http://workfutures.yk.ca/frames/f4/121_ey_4.htm

CLERICAL SUPERVISORS AND MANAGERS: http://stats.bls.gov/ocos127.htm

SAMPLE TECHNICAL COLLEGE INSTRUCTOR CERTIFICATION REQUIREMENTS: http://www.gateway. tec.wi.us/sub/campuses/employment/certification/initcert.htm

13
Telecommuting

LEARNING OBJECTIVES

- Explain two reasons why many transcription offices have switched to telecommuting
- List several differences between telecommuters and office-based employees
- Discuss several benefits of telecommuting to the employee
- Discuss the issue of productivity in the home environment
- List several ways in which a telecommuter can remain connected to his or her office and profession

ON-THE-JOB PROFILE
The Electronic Highway

In my office at the University of Washington we have about 40 very experienced medical transcriptionists. Presently over half of them are telecommuters working at home. I prefer to work in the office half-time and at home half-time. For the full-time office workers, it is quite sad as more and more colleagues "go home," even though we are glad they have this option. Between telecommuters and outside transcription services, more than two-thirds of the work is now done outside the office. This trend is widespread and will undoubtedly continue.

One of my favorite coworkers just "went home" a few weeks back, after working with us in the office for two years. Although I miss her a lot, I completely understand her preference. She lives an hour's drive away. Just the time saved in not driving will give her another 10 hours a week—not to mention saving her the expense and risk of travel. As Seattle is now ranked sixth nationally in highway congestion, it's a wonder anyone here commutes at all.

More and more, work in our society is being done on an electronic highway, often by telecommuters. In fact, this handbook grew out of an e-mail I received from my editor. Ninety percent of our business correspondence was accomplished by

ON-THE-JOB PROFILE   (continued)

e-mail. Similarly, most of my contact with the contributors to this book was via e-mail. That would not have been possible ten years ago—nor would most telecommuting exist without modern home computers.

A revolution is under way.

Telecommuters are a growing and increasingly important segment of the medical transcription profession. It would not surprise me if the entire industry were to become primarily home based in the future and increasingly more involved with the Internet.

That's all for now—gotta go check my e-mail!

With the advent of digital dictation equipment and sophisticated microcomputers, many office-based transcriptionists are switching to working at home. This major change has created a new type of employee: the telecommuting transcriptionist. The reasons for this change, the requirements of telecommuting, and its advantages and disadvantages should be thoroughly understood, not only by those contemplating such a change but also by office-based transcriptionists, to help them work more effectively with their home-based colleagues.

Many changes in the health care business are based on money—on attempts to cut costs (save money) or increase income (make money). Often both goals are pursued simultaneously. The technological reasons behind the rise of telecommuting among transcriptionists—more powerful home computers, faster modems, and sophisticated digital dictation systems—are secondary to the financial benefits to health care institutions. The belief is that having transcriptionists work out of their homes will save office overhead costs and enhance productivity. As many transcriptionists are taking advantage of this option, a brief overview is necessary to understand and analyze the pros and cons of telecommuting.

The hardware necessary for working at home as a telecommuter may be supplied by the employer or, at least partially, by the employee. The employer will have specific requirements concerning computer speed and memory, modem speed, and word processing programs and thus may prefer to supply the necessary equipment to ensure optimum performance and standardization of employee output. If equipment is supplied by the employer, the telecommuter should have homeowner's or renter's insurance that covers this equipment, for self-protection. Hardware provided by the employee, if permitted, may reduce the cost of initial office setup for the employer. Compensation to the employee for the use of such equipment, in the form of either a lease payment or a depreciation allowance, is negotiable.

Because of the high cost of digital dictation equipment, this should generally be provided by the employer. Professional installation of the dictation equipment is recommended and may be provided by the employer. In addition, the employer may require the employee to set up a "dedicated space" in the home where transcription is the only activity allowed. This could be an entire room or a portion of a room. Employees wishing to change to telecommuter status must understand and comply with such requirements.

Once the home work site is established and functioning, the process of telecommuting itself must be understood. The employee must keep to regular work hours, without direct supervision. Also, the lack of coworkers is a significant change from the office setting, reducing social distractions but also eliminating the support and interaction provided by fellow employees. A telecommuter must be able to focus on the work without direct encouragement, maintain a schedule independently, and possibly troubleshoot minor computer or modem difficulties without relying on in-house staff. Having prior transcribing experience sufficient to "fill in the blanks" as much as possible, without directly consulting coworkers, is essential. Knowledge of computer operating systems, modems, digital dictation systems, and software programs beyond the minimum will be necessary to maintain a smooth work flow.

Overall, a telecommuter acts as a stand-alone medical transcription unit, self-sufficient and self-disciplined, contributing to the whole yet autonomous. The relative isolation and independence of telecommuting may not be appropriate for every employee.

The benefits of telecommuting include the obvious elimination of transportation time and expense, which grows increasingly important in crowded urban areas, and the freedom from the expense and obligation of wearing any specific work attire. That is not to say that a telecommuter should not wear professional attire during working hours, only that doing so is not required. Taking meals at home instead of dining out also cuts costs. Being available to family members in the home will have great importance to parents.

Some studies have indicated an approximately 20 percent increase in productivity among telecommuters, compared with in-office transcriptionists. Several factors might explain this increase. First, a surprising amount of time is consumed during the office workday by personal interactions, breaks, and helping others with difficult dictations. Working with others naturally develops personal relationships, concern for their welfare, and discussion of significant events. Although this is a healthy and desirable outcome, such interactions can easily "run long," cutting into productivity. Few if any employers build 15 minutes of conversation into "nonproductive time," and two long conversations during an eight-hour day could reduce daily productivity by 7–8 percent. Telecommuters lack such social distractions. They also may feel more in control of their own fortunes and thus work more diligently than they might in an office.

Another factor in improved productivity may be the home setting itself. A telecommuter is likely to feel relaxed and comfortable in the home environment, with access to fresh air, more natural lighting, and the freedom to make necessary adjustments in the workplace for personal comfort and convenience.

To perform at the highest possible level, telecommuters should have extensive medical references available. These will include not only the latest editions of standard drug references, medical dictionaries, and specialty books but also personal lists of words already researched, current lists of abbreviations and surgical equipment, copies of difficult dictations, and even lists of homeopathic herbs and medicines. Access to and familiarity with medical Web sites is strongly recommended. Becoming a successful medical transcription telecommuter is an active process, in some ways more challenging than working in an office setting, yet preferable for many people.

However independent the telecommuter feels, regular interaction with the home office and the transcription profession should not be ignored. Using e-mail and attending monthly staff meetings will allow regular contact with other "teles" and office coworkers. Additionally, AAMT meetings may offer an expanded view of transcription, with opportunities to contribute to the profession as a whole.

By combining the cost savings and independence of working at home with active professional associations, the telecommuter may have the best of both worlds, maintaining an optimal work environment while keeping abreast of frequent changes affecting the profession.

SWITCHING FROM OFFICE TO HOME

Peggy Donaldson

It is very, very quiet working at my house. The pets just sleep all day, and there isn't much noise in the neighborhood (everyone's at work except the retirees). It is certainly a comfortable work setting, though, and there are no obstacles to getting a lot of work done. Unfortunately, this abrupt upgrade in my productivity means that my elbows and wrists are a little sore.

In my case, there wasn't much to do to become a telecommuter. The techs came over one day and brought my new equipment and set it up. All I had to do was provide the space in my home. The university provided the phone lines and even the chair and keyboard tray, too. The main difference in working at home is that there is no one to listen to a word when you need help. The resources are less extensive than in the office. And you get lonely, especially if you are used to seeing a lot of friends, and suddenly there is no one around you. You need to be self-sufficient and better at organizing getting together with people.

It seems extremely important to have the actual space you work in be conducive to working. I am lucky and don't have little ones at home to distract me. If a person does have small children and needs to work at home, it would be crucial to arrange working hours when someone else could watch the kids, or at night or very early in the morning when they are sleeping.

A big plus for me is having a window to look out of! My view is literally of a forest, so it's very peaceful, and that helps me feel good about working here. It is worth the effort to arrange a comfortable work space. I don't recommend working in a corner with no view.

Mini-breaks are very important, because when you have no distractions you type more and your body gets tired. Luckily, telecommuters have built-in breaks while waiting for the system to save jobs.

Finally, remember to stay in touch with the home office. If your equipment breaks down and you can't work, you'll need to know what to do and whom to

SWITCHING FROM OFFICE TO HOME   (continued)

call to get things fixed. You'll also need to stay current with changes in work-related procedures and policies. There should be someone at the main office who can answer your questions and help you get back on track if your system isn't working properly, or you are unclear about a new procedure. So read your e-mail, make those phone calls, and do whatever it takes to stay in the loop. "Out of sight, out of mind" is *not* a good motto for a telecommuter.

REVIEW QUESTIONS

1. Do employers ever supply computer hardware and transcription systems for telecommuters?
2. Is telecommuting an appropriate choice for every medical transcriptionist?
3. What medical references should a telecommuter have on hand?
4. Should a telecommuter have Internet access at home? Why or why not?
5. Does telecommuting usually increase or decrease overall productivity? Why?
6. Why should the telecommuter maintain regular contact with the transcription office?

RELATED WEB SITES

TELECOMMUTING NEWS STORIES ON THE NET: http://www.telecommute.org/news.html
TELECOMMUTING WEB SITE: http://www.sangabriel.com/tc.htm
NTI MEDICAL TRANSCRIPTION COURSE: http://caes.mit.edu/nc/nti/nti-medical/html
WORK FROM HOME JOBS DIGEST: http://www.intlhomeworkers.com/default.htm

14
Home-Based Transcription

LEARNING OBJECTIVES

- Explain three key benefits of home-based employment
- Compare the different social environments of home and office
- List several challenges for home workers
- Discuss interacting with family members while working at home
- Explain site location, computer hardware, and space requirements for the home office
- Discuss safety issues for the home-based transcriptionist

ON-THE-JOB PROFILE
On the Home Front

In 1983, before home businesses became so popular, I started my own small press. My first children's book sold three hundred copies in a few months, which seemed quite amazing at the time. Since then I've published 20 different poetry titles, with local and national mail order distribution. Over the years my home-based business endeavors have included making jewelry, performing on-line research, writing magazine articles, and now writing this handbook.

I've learned more about business from running my own for 15 years than I might have in a century working for someone else. Selling a product or service yourself gives you a great appreciation of what makes commerce tick. Those of you planning to transcribe at home, independently, have an opportunity to learn how the medical industry and business in general work. You will learn about making a business plan, marketing, sales, customer service, taxes, and record keeping—just to start. Planning and growing a business is an exciting process—riskier than being an employee but also more interesting and rewarding.

There are many opinions about what makes a successful home business. Certainly, having adequate financial resources to get started is advisable. Yet I

In the last few years, advances in technology and changes in health care delivery have
allowed many medical transcriptionists to work out of their own homes as self-
employed contractors. New transcription graduates may have the option, initially or after
a reasonable amount of "in-house" transcription experience, to manage their own home-
based transcription businesses.

After completing your medical transcription training, you must make a choice:
work in an office or work independently at home. There are many factors to weigh before making this decision, and carefully considering all the variables before choosing
is advisable. Charting the right course now will lay the groundwork for years of successful medical transcription.

Many students are attracted to transcription because it does allow people to work
at home. Parents with young children, especially, appreciate the prospect of working in
the home, being available to their children, and saving on child care costs. Those who
prefer to "run their own show" may also be attracted to the idea of independent medical
transcription.

There are several economic advantages to working at home. The first of these is
that there are no transportation expenses. The home worker saves the cost of a daily
drive to the office, parking, automobile expenses, or bus fare. Coupled with this savings is reduced stress and risk by avoiding driving in rush-hour traffic. A 30-minute
commute each way, five days a week, equals 5 hours a week, or 250 hours per year.
Commuting 10 miles each way for five days every week, at an average of 30 cents per
mile, entails an annual cost of $1,500!

Another work-related expense is the cost of food purchased during the workday.
Although it is certainly possible to bring a lunch to work, many office workers eat at
least some meals out during the average work week. Snacks and soft drinks add to these
expenses. Buying only two lunches weekly, at $5 each, and five snack items weekly,
also totaling $5, would add up to $750 per year. The combination of transportation and
food expenses, therefore, can easily exceed $2,000 annually.

A third work-related expense is the cost of business clothing. Home workers may
not require professional business attire unless clients are coming over. This represents
a potentially significant savings on dress clothes, shoes, dry cleaning, and the time and
transportation it takes to shop for and maintain clothing.

If day care is required for small children, the cost savings provided by working at
home can be significant—up to $150 or more per week!

On a personal level, there are advantages to working alone at home rather than
with others in an office. The lack of distractions found in an office can raise individual

productivity. With no one to discuss the day's events with, focusing on the work at hand is often easier. Since medical transcription is production oriented, the 20 minutes a day not spent talking with coworkers could translate, over an eight-hour shift, into a 5 percent increase in productivity. Those workers paid by the line will receive an immediate financial gain from this.

Similarly, not having to share a desk, as happens in many busy offices, may lead to greater efficiency. Once a home worker sets up his or her desk and computer to best advantage, they stay that way. Home workers also have more control over their working hours, since desk space doesn't have to be available for a coworker at a certain time. The organized, stable home-based desktop reduces distractions and time wasted rearranging. Lighting, chair height, keyboard angle, and other settings can be customized for individual preference.

Another significant, yet perhaps overlooked, benefit of home employment is environmental quality. Modern office buildings have heating and ventilation systems but lack windows that open for fresh air. With the advent of computers, copiers, and overcrowding, office air quality has declined. Airborne pathogens transmitted between coworkers may adversely affect employee health. Space requirements in busy health care facilities may also cause the relocation of transcription departments to less desirable internal locations, even to the basement.

The home worker, conversely, has the option to open a window for fresh air, step outside, and generally feel more connected to the natural environment, and he or she avoids the respiratory ailments circulated in offices. Over time, good environmental conditions may significantly promote personal health.

A key word to summarize the advantages of home-based transcription might be *freedom.* The home worker has a greater degree of personal freedom, no coworkers to contend with, and the flexibility to adapt the workplace to satisfy individual style and needs. Combined with economic advantages, the enhanced freedom afforded by home-based medical transcription is a powerful incentive for working at home.

To balance this equation, however, the disadvantages of working at home merit equal consideration. The first of these is the self-motivation necessary to manage personal freedom. It takes discipline to get up early and start working without a time clock or supervisor hovering nearby. Sticking to one's tasks and hours without external controls may be difficult for some individuals. Knowing one's own nature is important before making the move to work at home.

Second, working at home often means working alone. Especially for the newer transcriptionist, this will be challenging. Not only are there no coworkers to socialize with, there is no experienced coworker at hand to consult when a word is unclear. Inevitable problems with dictation, such as mumbling, improper word usage, background noise, and unfamiliar accents, often require experienced ears to decipher. Newer transcriptionists planning to work at home should arrange a "safety net" of other transcriptionists to provide necessary assistance with difficult dictations. Nor should possible feelings of isolation from working alone be discounted; what might be a blessing to some could be a problem for others.

When working in the home, interactions with family members will need to be carefully handled. To allow proper work flow and adequate production, the difference between important family business and casual interruptions must be clarified. Althoug "family time" will vary with each household, limits must be set for work to be con pleted. Setting guidelines before switching to home-based transcription, and having re ular meetings with family members, will help the work-at-home employee manage far ily relationships with fewer inappropriate interruptions.

Another, perhaps less obvious, disadvantage of working at home concerns soci status and attitudes. In our society, great emphasis is placed on working, and offices a the primary locations for that work. The home environment may have less credibility th the customary workplace. Just as "homemakers" raising a family have been given le credit than they deserve, transcriptionists working at home may perceive a loss of stat in the eyes of others. Similarly, being self-employed can make it more difficult to obta credit. Also, self-employment taxes require a broader understanding of income taxatic tax forms, and allowable deductions. Professional tax assistance may be necessary.

Finally, a disadvantage of some significance is that of "being out of the loop Without regular trips to the office, the home worker is subtly disenfranchised. Offi politics and rumors are not known. Changes in management styles and thinking may missed. Opportunities for promotion and advancement (such as to lead transcription or even office manager) may be weighted in favor of those who work in the offic Workers wishing to move up in an organization would do well to keep these possibi ties in mind before deciding to work at home. It's hard to score a home run when you' out in left field.

Considering all the pros and cons of home-based employment prior to setting shop is one major factor in making an informed decision. It also makes sense to an lyze the positive and negative aspects of working in an office, to fully appreciate t best possible course of action.

The first advantage in working on site, in an office, is access to experience. Tra scriptionists working together in an office routinely share information and help one a other. They may share word processing tips, discuss proper formats, distribute cop of difficult dictations, help coworkers with unusual physician names, or listen to u clear words or phrases encountered by a colleague. The value of this resource, es cially to a newer transcriptionist, is significant.

Like most people, dictating health care providers tend to speak in patterns, reus standard phrases. They often talk faster and less clearly when uttering phrases they' used a hundred times. Experienced coworkers are familiar with these speech patte and can often clarify tangled phrases.

Also, many transcriptionists keep samples of difficult dictations on file to av reinventing the wheel. Access to experienced, professional transcriptionists can si plify and speed the work flow.

Similarly, experienced transcriptionists may have information on local AAN chapters and are often well acquainted with working conditions and pay scales at near health care institutions. Moonlighting, or working after hours for other organizatio is quite common among transcriptionists. Experienced coworkers may know the b places to secure "extracurricular" employment.

A second advantage of working in a transcription office is the availability of me ical reference books. Transcription offices generally provide medical dictionaries a pharmacology references, and they may also have specialty term books, surgical reference books, and directories of physicians and hospitals. This can save the office worker the cost of having to purchase these fairly expensive books individually. In addition, some transcriptionists bring their personal reference collections to work and allow coworkers access to them.

The third advantage of working in an office is on-site management. Transcription supervisors can monitor individual progress and make specific suggestions for improvement. Their experience can be valuable in guiding the newer transcriptionist toward optimum production and high quality. Also, procedural questions can be immediately referred up to the supervisor, in person.

Quality assurance is likewise an issue directly related to choice of employment sites. The goal of medical transcription is to approach 100 percent accuracy on every report. Maintaining the highest possible quality may be easier with ready access to coworkers' and supervisors' input regarding perplexing or incomprehensible dictations. Frequent feedback, as well as opportunities to participate in quality assessment, can provide the in-house medical transcriptionist with higher-quality output and learning opportunities.

Working in an office often provides the opportunity to obtain "inside information" unavailable to the home worker. Such information may pop up in conversations, in break-room discussions, in memos, on posted flyers, and in many other ways. Often it's just a casual bit of information, such as a change in someone's status or a new policy, but having an ear to the ground is always worthwhile.

As mentioned earlier, on-site workers are generally favored when it comes to promotions. In a two-tiered organization, with both on-site and at-home workers, those closer to the decision makers may be more likely to advance. This is due to a combination of closer interpersonal relationships, closer monitoring of organizational changes and needs, and possibly the greater perceived dedication and involvement of the in-office worker. The inner circle often gets rewarded first. The extremities, or home workers, may be the last to know.

The disadvantages of working in a transcription office must also be closely evaluated. Perhaps the most familiar downside to working on site is office politics. In any group of workers, a certain amount of politics is unavoidable. Many people strive for advancement in their organization or to influence others or affect the outcomes of various situations. Working in the office setting requires interacting with others on multiple levels, both social and professional. Although the intensity and nature of office politics will vary from office to office, it will always be a factor to be dealt with.

Interpersonal distractions are another consideration when working in the office. Many people like to talk at work, and an excess of talk can lower production. Also, clerks and other nontranscriptionists may not appreciate the dedication needed to achieve one's required line count. Transcriptionists are human, too, and naturally converse with others in the office. A certain amount of such interaction is healthy and enjoyable. However, the home transcriptionist is usually freed from this type of distraction, and his or her production may rise accordingly.

In the traditional office setting, time is more highly regulated than it may be at home. Employees are expected to work set hours. This allows management to control the work flow more readily, but it also confines the office worker to a specific schedule. Working at home, especially when self-employed, lends flexibility to one's schedule. As many, or more, hours of work may be performed as in an office, but management of those hours rests with the transcriptionist. This additional control over one's lifestyle has substantial value, especially when scheduling appointments and personal business.

The added costs of office employment, as mentioned previously, could be a deciding factor for some transcriptionists. The opportunity to save up to several thousand dollars a year on transportation, dining out, and work attire could be the equivalent of making an additional dollar per hour in salary for a full-time transcriptionist. Those who are paid by the line and are able to enhance their production due to reduced distractions and socializing might profit even more. The independent transcriptionist can also more readily adopt new technologies, as he or she need not wait for an organizational decision to do so.

By reviewing and evaluating major differences between home and office employment, the best individual decision can be made. However, several variations on standard full-time employment should also be noted and considered. Part-time employment in the office, combined with working part-time at home, could expand an employee's flexibility while still maintaining a close connection with the central organization. Part-time second-shift, weekend, or even nighttime work might allow similar advantages. After regular business hours, office conditions tend to be more relaxed. The part-time or evening worker can avoid most office politics yet still have access to vital information. Also, workers who fill less desirable weekend or evening shifts may earn an extra measure of job security.

Once the decision has been made to work outside the office, a variety of options need to be studied. The first is whether to locate your work space on or off your own personal property. There are advantages to both options, which will vary with individual needs and situations. Of note: Once a location has been selected, changing it will be difficult. Great care should therefore be taken in selecting the location process, with the goal of acquiring at least a semipermanent business-ready location.

Working outside the home but not in a formal transcription office can mean renting private office space, leasing a portion of someone else's property, or sharing office space with other independent transcriptionists. If renting space, it should be conveniently located and economical, to avoid overhead costs' consuming too much income. Having a private office, if affordable, can be an asset when entertaining clients. An office lends credibility, particularly if regular hours are kept. At the same time, control of working hours remains with the individual. A private space allows the necessary freedom from distractions to achieve optimum production.

If a private office is not financially viable, leasing an unused yet appropriate space, such as an outbuilding, garage apartment, or separate section of someone else's home, is a second option. This lease can be entered into individually or shared with other independent transcriptionists. The advantage of this option is that it provides a dedicated work space and avoids the problems associated with merging home and office. This option may also allow easier expansion if and when additional contracts are obtained.

Adapting existing outbuildings adjacent to one's home is another consideration. There may be semifinished garage space, portable buildings, or a garage apartment that can easily be converted into a home office. Taking advantage of incompletely used accessory space could provide an autonomous yet highly convenient transcription site.

If you do decide to locate your work space within your home, a "paradigm shift," or change in thinking, may be in order. Suddenly your place of rest and relaxation is also where you go to work. Much like doing market research before locating a new store, analyzing the home is a prerequisite for successful self-employment.

Ideally, you should dedicate a separate room to your medical transcription office. Realistically, such a generous portion of unclaimed space may be unlikely. The focus, therefore, should be on identifying the most functional space, then adapting the household to accommodate home employment. The identification process can proceed room by room, emphasizing existing vacant space, or space that could be freed up with minimal adaptations. Incorporating family members' opinions in this process is a good idea. The designated space must be large enough to contain the transcriptionist's desk and chair, a computer system, a printer, a transcriber, a phone, chairs for clients, a fax machine, and file cabinets. Like all businesses, room to expand, as files grow and technology advances, should be anticipated. For your own health and comfort, allow enough room to move freely in your chair and interview clients, as well as access to adequate natural light and fresh air.

A home traffic analysis may contribute to effective location of the office. Like cities, homes have regular traffic patterns, with resultant variations in noise and congestion. Just as a home buyer might avoid a street fronting the local airport, the home-based transcriptionist should stay away from the noisiest and busiest portions of the house. A quiet and orderly work space will generate the best results. Also, time of day may be directly related to household traffic; if possible, transcription hours could be adjusted accordingly.

Sharing a room within the home may be necessary. If so, the other activities that take place in the shared room must be compatible with the home business. For example, combining a home gym or laundry room with a transcription office would be a bad idea, but sharing space with a household library or a second home worker would be fine. Room dividers may be useful in defining and isolating the work space. Regular working hours will also tend to reinforce the serious purpose of the home office.

As mentioned, planning for expansion during the initial phase of home office development is advisable. Records of clients, work completed, and work pending; business-related receipts; networking files; medical and business information downloaded from the Internet; business plans and updates—records of every kind will need to be filed and maintained. Upgrades in computer hardware and software as well as peripheral technologies such as digital dictation systems may require additional space. Planning for success implies leaving room for gradual expansion, and an initial scarcity of workspace will soon require adjustments.

In conjunction with the space identification process, an assessment of the interaction between home office and family members is also necessary. Incorporating a work site into the home, if a new process, is a major change.

Family members, especially children, will need to understand how they will be affected by the home office. Rules for interaction during work hours, for noise control, and for appropriate and inappropriate interruptions must be made clear. The advantages and opportunities of home employment can be pointed out. Benefits to the family, both short- and long-term, should be discussed and understood.

Like most enterprises, a home-based business is a cooperative venture. It relies on the efforts and goodwill of all participants to flourish. Defining the work space and work requirements is only half the battle. Of much greater value is including family members and/or roommates in the process of creating a home business. Sharing the plans, the excitement, and the day-to-day achievements allows the family to adjust to and appreciate the change to working at home.

SETTING UP THE HOME OFFICE

The next phase of setting up a home office, once the location is decided, should be interviewing and research. This can take the form of interviewing home-based medical transcriptionists working either as employees or independents. It may also mean researching office supplies, furniture, computer hardware and software—not just to get the best immediate price and quality but also to establish long-term, positive relationships with suppliers.

Contacting home-based medical transcriptionists could be accomplished by calling community or technical colleges that offer courses in medical transcription, contacting hospital transcription departments, checking Yellow Pages listings, consulting the MT Daily or similar Web sites, or calling the local chapter of AAMT.

Meeting home-based transcriptionists will provide the opportunity to see working home-based offices, ask questions, take notes, and better understand the style and functionality necessary for a successful office. Similarly, discussing the many aspects of MT work—such as production, quality assurance, fees, business records, and computers—with experienced home-based transcriptionists will be invaluable.

Compensating these people for their valuable time is appropriate. Keep thorough records of any transcriptionists met in this manner and mail follow-up thank you notes. Thereafter, periodic calls may provide future employment opportunities for vacation or overflow coverage.

In addition to conducting personal interviews, performing general research about home-based business is also valuable. The trend toward working at home has inspired many home-based employment handbooks, with basic information often applicable to home-based medical transcriptionists. Additionally, studying sales and marketing handbooks may benefit the transcriptionist new to self-employment. The general rules of customer service and business etiquette apply equally to all entrepreneurs. Self-employed transcriptionists will soon discover they have replaced one supervisor (in the transcription office) with many (each customer). Building a solid basis in business, enhanced by courtesy and sincerity, will increase the chances of success. Learning about contracts for transcription services (see box) is also necessary.

Contract for Medical Transcription Services

This contract is made and entered into on _____ (date) by
_____ (herein called the client) whose
address is _____,
and _____, (your name), (herein called the contractor), whose address is _____,
(your address). In consideration of the mutual promises in this contract, the
parties agree to abide by all the terms of this contract. It is understood that the
contractor is an independent contractor and not an employee of the client and
therefore will be responsible for all taxes and withholdings.

Contractor agrees to do the following: medical transcription in accordance with
the client's documentation guidelines and forms. Services shall include:

1. Pickup and delivery of dictated and transcribed tapes
2. Transcription in accordance with the client's documentation guidelines and
   form
3. Providing full confidentiality of transcribed material
4. Availability for questions and consultation on an as-needed basis via phone
   or in person
5. Forty-eight-hour turnaround from the time transcription is made available
   to me, unless otherwise specified
6. Billing invoice provided by contractor twice monthly (due the 1st and the
   15th of the month)
7. Providing plain paper printing for transcription, with the understanding that
   any special paper or letterhead will be provided by the client
8. Providing professional service and demeanor to the client at all times
9. Providing extra copies at a rate of $.50 fee per page

Pickup and delivery of the materials needed to complete this service will be made
by the contractor, or her appointed courier, at the client's place of business at such
a time agreed upon by both the contractor and the client. Client agrees to have
tapes ready for pickup at the time agreed upon by contractor and client. Tapes that
are not ready or changes in schedule that cause the contractor to have to schedule
additional pickups will result in a $.30 per mile fee.

Contractor promises that the final product will be completed to the client's satisfaction.

For performing the work described above, client agrees to pay the contractor the
amount of _____ per line. It is agreed that according to the definition stated

Contract for Medical Transcription Services (continued)

by the AAMT, sixty-five (65) characters constitute a line. STAT transcription may be available at a rate of $1\frac{1}{2} \times$ normal rate per line and is subject to an (as available basis).

Either party may terminate this contractual agreement (termination must be submitted in writing) on not less than 30 days' notice. However, repeated failure to provide transcription on a timely basis on the part of the contractor, breech of confidentiality statement on the part of the contractor, or failure to comply with timely payments on the part of the client may result in immediate termination of this contract. This must be submitted in writing. At the time of termination any and all materials belonging to the client must be and will be returned, and any and all completed transcription by the contractor must be paid for, in full. Contract will be considered still in effect until all monies owed to contractor are paid in full.

Confidentiality: As a contractor, it is the contractor's responsibility not to violate any confidence of the patient or their family through indiscriminate discussion pertaining to patients, their treatment, diagnosis, or progress. Erroneous and non-public information released by contractor shall result in legal liability.

The contractor understands and agrees that all patient records and patient information are strictly confidential and will not make any disclosures.

Errors and Omissions Insurance: It is the contractor's policy that the computer-authenticated or other artificial signatures generated by means other than the actual dictating physician's signature are not endorsed by the contractor. Therefore the doctors should proofread their transcription for document content, accuracy, and quality control.

No changes shall be made in this agreement unless those changes are agreed to in writing by the contractor and by the client.

The initial investigation of office supplies and equipment should be preceded by a thorough home business inventory. Desks, chairs, and computer equipment already owned may reduce start-up expenses. Lower-cost substitutes, such as plastic filing cases instead of expensive metal filing cabinets, may be initially acceptable. Although proper equipment is certainly desirable, funds saved by using inexpensive substitutes can be applied to grow the business. This strategy may help reduce business expenses until sufficient accounts can be developed.

To obtain the best possible price and value for materials received, a combination of three factors is suggested. This is based on the concepts that prices for the same item can vary greatly; levels of quality can vary; and prices, no matter how plainly marked or firmly supported, may be negotiable.

Calling multiple office suppliers with a list of desired items and comparing prices will suggest the best general office supply source. Different suppliers may have better prices on different items. Large items such as computers and office furniture should be carefully researched. Look also for included warranties, on-site service departments, and relative cost and length of service contracts, if desired, to provide maintenance of major purchases. Striking a balance between low cost and convenient location will streamline repairs when necessary. *There is no guarantee that higher price ensures higher quality.* Look for a combination of intrinsic quality (sturdiness and durability, ease of use, simplicity) and product warranties included in the price. Inspect each item before purchasing it, to avoid wasting time on unnecessary returns. This means opening sealed cartons before exiting the store, to ensure that all required parts are included.

The higher the price of an item, the more potential there is for negotiation. The standard for many retail items is the "keystone," or 100 percent, markup. Goods that cost $100 wholesale are thus sold for $200 retail. This allows the retailer to discount sale merchandise up to 50 percent (from $200 down to $100) without incurring a loss. Although not all merchandise is "keystoned," all merchandise does have a built-in profit margin. Offering less than the quoted, or list, price on large ticket items, combined with a willingness to give and take, may secure unexpected discounts. Purchasing multiple items at the same time may provide more leverage.

Timing can be an integral part of negotiating. Time major purchases for late in the lowest-volume sales day (often Monday), when salespersons may be more anxious for a sale, or near closing, when quotas may not have been reached. Making major purchases near the end of any month, or in January, a traditionally slow sales month, may yield substantial discounts. Cost savings obtained in this way can be applied to sustaining and developing the new business.

The issue of new versus used office equipment also deserves mention. Durable items such as desks and filing cabinets, in good condition, may be far more economical used, without any loss of function. More complex purchases, such as computers, require caution and knowledge to purchase on a used basis. Also, limited or nonexistent warranties on used computers add to the risk if problems arise. If purchasing a new system is out of reach, leasing is an alternative to buying a used system.

Setting up and arranging the home office involves a number of separate considerations, including electrical requirements, safety, environmental issues, lighting, furniture, computers, reference books, licenses, taxes, and business practices. These are discussed in the following paragraphs.

Electrical Requirements

Have an adequate number of grounded, three-pronged electrical outlets in the work area for all necessary electrical appliances. Surge protectors are required to guard sensitive computer equipment. Avoid extension cords and plug adapters. Test operations to be sure household circuits are not overloaded. Consult an electrician if needed.

Safety

Check to be sure paths are clear, with no electrical cords protruding. Have a fire extinguisher readily accessible, and install a smoke alarm in the room. Be sure fire exits are unblocked. Store business records in fire-resistant containers when possible. Allow adequate room for chair movement and client visits.

Environment

Take advantage of the freedom of working at home by allowing maximal fresh air into your work space. Provide attractive plants, art work for the walls, and other personal touches to enhance the overall effect. Regular dusting and vacuuming, combined with natural ventilation, will reduce the likelihood of illness or allergies and promote good health.

Lighting

In an office setting, fluorescent lights are the norm due to their relatively low cost. However, the home worker can choose incandescent bulbs, a better and less flickering light source. Have adequate lighting for your work space, testing different wattage bulbs for personal preference. In daytime hours, combine natural light with artificial light. Avoid glare on computer monitors. Adjust monitor brightness and contrast settings as necessary. Experiment for optimal workplace lighting, which will vary with different rooms. Remember to keep delicate computer equipment out of direct sunlight. Moveable lamps, such as architects use, will add flexibility to lighting choices.

Furniture

Your desk or desks will be the primary focus of your transcription operation. A good used desk is fairly economical and a more efficient use of space than a table. Look for adequate size and sturdiness; check drawers for depth. Obtain a large bottom drawer if files will be stored in the desk. Be sure drawers move smoothly in and out and knobs or handles are secure. Measure desktop length, width, and desk height before purchasing computer equipment, to avoid mismatches. Sit at the desk to gauge leg room, turning room in a swivel chair, and desktop height for comfort. Try out two desks paired in an L-shape.

Before shopping, diagram the configuration of computer and transcription equipment to ensure adequate desktop space. Check the legs of the desk for sturdiness. Be sure any desks purchased will fit through existing door frames in the home.

At least one filing cabinet and one bookcase should be placed adjacent to the desk. Files must be readily accessible when phoning, and alphabetically or subjectively organized. Bookcases may contain not only medical and general references but also computer manuals and Internet references and resources. Files and book collections are almost guaranteed to grow as the business evolves. Organization and regular file maintenance will reduce access time for information.

The transcriptionist's chair requires adjustable height, adequate back support, comfort, and durability. The longer the working hours, the more important a comfortable yet supportive chair will be.

A chair with variable heights is important for several reasons. Adjusting the chair height periodically during the work shift adjusts the body position to help reduce fatigue. Different chair heights will allow different positioning of the transcriber foot pedal, again reducing fatigue. Transcriptionists who sit for eight or more hours at a stretch need variations in position, as well as breaks and stretching, to promote good circulation. The chair back should also be adjustable, to move farther forward or backward from the workstation. Good posture as well as varied positions will promote good health.

The science of ergonomics, or body mechanics, will be helpful in setting up the transcription workspace. This science—sometimes called human engineering—seeks the optimum positions and least harmful motions in the workplace. Applications of ergonomics to transcription include adjusting the height of the computer monitor to eye level; varying the height and angle of the keyboard to avoid repetitive-motion injuries; varying the chair, as mentioned previously; finding an optimal foot pedal position and changing the pedal periodically from the left leg to the right; and arranging files, bookcases, and furniture for easy access. Taking care of the transcriptionist is just as important as organizing the transcription work site. The overall design and function of the work space, carefully conceived, will contribute not only to the best possible work output but also to the safety, health, and enjoyment of the home-based medical transcriptionist.

Computers

To be able to run continuous voice-recognition software as well as word processing and expander programs requires, at a minimum, a 166 MHz Pentium computer with at least 32 megabytes of RAM. A faster processor (200 MHz or more) and 64 megabytes of RAM is even better. Lower-priced used computers will allow basic word processing but will soon require upgrades or replacement. Obtaining the best affordable equipment will directly relate to optimal output. A larger, 17-inch monitor, rather than the usual 13- to 15-inch size, will provide easier viewing. Include a CD-ROM drive (16× or faster) and a rapid modem (56.6K or higher) for Internet access.

Software programs should include widely used operating systems such as Windows 95, 98, or 2000 and professional word processing software such as Microsoft Word for Windows or Corel WordPerfect. Also, previous versions of these programs, particularly WordPerfect 5.1, are still widely used by some transcription departments. Word-expansion software programs may enhance productivity for a reasonable cost (generally under $200).

Since an independent transcriptionist may have multiple clients with different needs, the ability to transcribe both minicassettes and microcassettes is advised. This allows immediate acceptance and delivery of contract work without having to seek more appropriate equipment. Transcribing from tapes is the easiest and most affordable route to start with; however, it does require pickup and delivery of tapes on a regular basis. The use of rerecording equipment or a digital dictation system may require working with a transcription service that will provide this more costly equipment.

Reference Books

The at-home transcriptionist's reference library is of paramount importance. These books provide the necessary information to complete reports. Current editions of a medical dictionary, a formulary, and surgical and other specialty references are the minimum needed to set up shop. In addition, supplemental word lists can be downloaded from World Wide Web sites. Maintaining a list of unfamiliar words encountered, with correct spellings and meanings, will save time in the future. Skillful reference use will leave more time free for generating income.

Fees and Licensing

In addition to acquiring the physical components of the home office, the business aspects need prompt attention. State, county, and city business licenses may be required. Zoning regulations regarding home businesses should be investigated. Besides performing transcription, the independent transcriptionist must obtain and manage accounts and keep thorough, organized records. Writing a formal business plan is a step toward operating a successful transcription business and will help in securing start-up capital, if needed. It may take months to develop sufficient contracts to cover business and living expenses. Do you have adequate cash or credit reserves to cover months of low income? Obtaining bank or family loans, or lines of credit, before opening an independent business is prudent. Projecting anticipated income and costs for the first year of operation can provide a guide to realistic financial management.

Managing marketing and "housekeeping" time is an important consideration for an independent contractor. How much time should be spent actively securing business through mailings, phone calls, and personal visits to health care facilities? Ten hours per week spent seeking jobs and keeping records leaves only 30 hours per full-time week for actual transcription.

In the beginning, considerable time must be allocated to obtaining accounts. This amount of time will vary with individual circumstances. This is nonproductive time, and financial projections should include it as a cost of marketing.

Taxes

For those new to self-employment, additional knowledge of federal and state income taxes will be needed. Self-employed workers must keep track of business-related expenditures in order to deduct them on their Schedule C (Net Profit from Business). A good working knowledge of taxation will allow the new business owner to take all legitimate deductions and thus improve profitability. The self-employed must also file Schedule SE (Self-Employment Tax). Seeking professional tax preparation may be advisable at first.

Business Practices

Marketing the business may take many forms, and techniques may vary in effectiveness in different communities. The basic tools of letterhead, business cards, and attractive brochures present a business in a professional manner. Business announcements or flyers can be sent or hand-delivered to specific health care providers and institutions in the vicinity, with follow-up phone calls. Brochures may indicate credentials, reliability, rapid turn around times, and other desirable features.

Complimentary tape pickup and report delivery will provide convenience for busy, cost-conscious providers. The transcription service can be advertised via bulletin boards in health care facilities, in local newspapers and weeklies, by word of mouth, and in local health-oriented publications. Brief personal visits to drop off brochures and request an appointment emphasize direct customer service and interest.

Establishing fees is one of the more challenging aspects of setting up a transcription business. Fees must be related to the level of income required, the amount customers will perceive as fair, and current community standards. Researching fees charged by other local home-based transcriptionists is useful, but these contractors may be reluctant to share their fee schedules with a potential competitor. Community contacts, such as those made at AAMT meetings or health-related seminars, may help a newly independent transcriptionist gather information on fees.

For example, a transcriptionist who averages 120 lines per hour and charges 12 cents per line will have a gross average income of $14.40 per hour. After business operating costs and taxes, the net income may be only $10 per hour. In some states this is an acceptable wage; in larger urban areas it is inadequate, however. Changing from 12 cents per line to 15 cents per line, if compatible with local standards, would increase the gross income to $18 per hour, or approximately $13 per hour net—a more acceptable income. Similarly, raising the rate to 15 cents per line and also improving productivity to 140 lines per hour would generate $21 per hour gross, or approximately $16 per hour net. For a 40-hour week, subtracting 10 hours for nonproductive time, that would yield a net income of $480 per week for 30 hours of actual transcribing. Finding the right combination of fees and productivity improvements will involve trial and error. Once a fee is established with a client, raising it may require considerable negotiation. Setting fees too low inhibits the chance for financial success. Setting fees too high will discourage new business. Transcriptionists whose workload expands beyond their abilities may eventually hire subcontractors and profit from the labor of others as well as their own.

In addition to seeking individual contracts, an independent transcriptionist may also place bids for overflow work at transcription offices and services or offer to help other independent MTs with their overflow. This work may require knowledge of specific word processing programs or medical records programs, such as Intelus. Overflow work may be seasonal or temporary and include vacation or illness back-up for other independents. Such short-term contracts may lead to more extensive opportunities later on. Also, having several running contracts reduces the impact if one account is cancelled.

It should be noted that independent work may require evening or weekend hours, as contract turnaround times dictate. The security of a 9-to-5 daytime position is exchanged for the flexibility, higher income potential, and, sometimes, longer hours of the self-employed MT.

While developing the business, regular networking and community interaction can be considered a low-cost form of advertising. Attending transcription meetings, medical seminars, and community functions (always with business cards and brochures in hand), enables the independent transcriptionist to explain the service provided, offer further information or a site visit, and request additional contacts who might be interested in the service. Being active in the local medical and service communities, as time permits, means having greater visibility and thus greater potential to attract new business. As the service grows, contacts with other home-based MTs may provide reciprocal arrangements for vacation, illness, and overflow coverage.

Another critical task for success, in addition to *obtaining* accounts, is *maintaining* them. A monthly call to each account to inquire about their satisfaction and any unmet needs demonstrates concern. Prompt follow-up and correction of specific problems is always indicated, but so is the occasional note thanking the client for his or her business and requesting suggestions for improvement.

In summary, operating an independent medical transcription business requires a combination of transcribing and business skills. The personal freedom and income potential possible are directly tied to the marketing, transcribing, and business management abilities of the individual. In addition, benefit and tax obligations are transferred from the health care employer to the individual contractor, making record keeping and careful self-management essential for success.

REVIEW QUESTIONS

1. What are three economic advantages of working at home instead of in an office?
2. Why could working in a home office be likely to increase productivity?
3. How could working at home affect the chances for promotion?
4. Why is planning for expansion while setting up the home office advisable?
5. When purchasing materials, what three factors may affect price and value?
6. How can timing affect major office equipment purchases?
7. What factors will influence the setting of fees by an independent transcriptionist?

RELATED WEB SITES

WORKING AT HOME WITH CHILDREN: http://mtdaily.com/mtl/children.html

AAMT TIP SHEET FOR BECOMING A SELF-EMPLOYED MEDICAL TRANSCRIPTIONIST: http://www.aamt.org/selfemp.htm

MOTHERS HOME-BASED NETWORK: http://mhbn.com

HOME BUSINESS INSTITUTE: http://www.hbiweb.com

HOME OFFICE ASSOCIATION OF AMERICA: http://www.hoaa.com

NATIONAL ASSOCIATION OF HOME-BASED BUSINESSES: http://www.usahomebusiness.com

15
The Internet for Medical Transcriptionists

LEARNING OBJECTIVES

- List three general search engines on the World Wide Web
- List four employment-related World Wide Web sites
- Discuss several types of information available to medical transcriptionists on the Internet
- Explain opportunities for independent contracting available on the World Wide Web

ON-THE-JOB PROFILE
A Day in the Life of the Internet

In early 1998 my wife was the staff development coordinator for a small local hospital that did not yet have Internet access. I worked as an occasional volunteer in her office and had set up a modest medical library for the hospital.

On receiving several new and complex patients, the nursing staff sent an information request regarding methicillin-resistant Staphylococcus aureus (MRSA). They needed to know how to handle this difficult organism, right away. My wife called me at home, and I jumped on the Web.

Because of the technical nature of the information required, I chose the Medsearch World Wide Web site as my starting point. Within two hours I was able to find a significant amount of information on MRSA. I printed out at least 50 pages of relevant articles and delivered the appropriate information to my wife at the hospital. She checked it, set it up in a notebook, and took it directly to the floor. The nursing staff were then able to review the information and incorporate it into their operations.

This small example hints at the tremendous informational power of the Internet, which can provide each individual with a "virtual library" right at home. As both technology and transcription continue to evolve, I hope the two find common ground to better serve the medical community and support patient care.

Both new and veteran medical transcriptionists have a tremendous new resource at their disposal: the World Wide Web section of the Internet. For a moderate monthly fee, home computer users can subscribe to an on-line service, such as America Online, which provides electronic mail (e-mail), a variety of information and entertainment channels, and full World Wide Web access. Many other Internet service providers (ISPs) provide Internet access only, often at reduced cost or with fewer users per modem. Employers have the option to connect to the Internet and offer e-mail and medical research services to transcriptionists and health care providers. For those who do not yet own a home computer, public libraries provide Internet access for free and selected businesses provide access on a rental basis.

The World Wide Web uses a system of "addresses," called universal resource locators (URLs), to locate individual Web "sites" consisting of one or more Web "pages." Each individual Web site and page has a unique URL. The URL for the MT Daily site's "home page" is http://www.mtdaily.com.

The *http* stands for "hypertext transfer protocol." The hypertext protocol is what gives the Web its special ability to link highlighted words or phrases in one document to other, related documents. Clicking on a hypertext link, using a mouse, connects the user to the related page, which might be part of the same site as the original page or a page on an entirely different site.

The *WWW* in the URL, obviously, stands for "World Wide Web." Then, *mtdaily* is the "domain" name of the individual Web site. The suffix *com* stands for "commercial." Other standard suffixes include *gov* for "government," *edu* for "educational institution," and *org* for "organization." More suffixes are being added as the Web expands.

There are at least four distinct areas in which to search for medical transcription positions on-line. The first are the general "search engines," sites such as Yahoo, Lycos, Excite, Alta Vista, Hotbot, and Infoseek. These can be accessed through the following URLs:

> http://www.yahoo.com
> http://www.lycos.com
> http://www.excite.com
> http://www.altavista.com
> http://www.hotbot.com
> http://www.infoseek.com

Search engines allow the user to type in a specific word or words (a "search string"), such as "medical jobs" or even "medical transcription jobs," and receive lists of related Web pages. General search engines often return thousands of responses, with the most relevant pages listed first. Searches can be refined if satisfactory results are not obtained.

The next area is general job-related databases. Major Web sites for job information and resume posting, which may contain medical opportunities, include the following:

1. http://www.jobhunt.com
2. http://www.monster.com
3. http://www.careermosaic.com
4. http://www.adamsonline.com

These general job sites often include valuable information on cover letters, resume preparation, and on-line resume submission. Also, different sites, both general and specifically medical, may have different jobs listed, so all may be worth investigating during on-line searches.

Job sites specific to medical careers include the following:

1. http://www.medjobs.com
2. http://www.jobsinmedicine.com
3. http://www.medsearch.com
4. http://www.medhunters.com
5. http://www.healthopps.com
6. http://www.hcjobsonline.com

As the Internet develops, it is likely that more and more positions will be offered on-line. Positions that require Internet knowledge, for whatever reason, may only be offered on-line. (Although this is not yet the case with medical transcription, changes must be anticipated.) As medical career sites increase in number, a preliminary site search through a general search engine, or using a reference such as the *Internet Yellow Pages* or *Web Bound Quarterly,* may generate the most comprehensive job site listings. *Web Bound Quarterly,* a journal available at major bookstores, has a particularly extensive list of career-related sites under their "Employment" and "Health" subject headings; also, check on-line listings and links.

A fourth area is Web sites of specific major health care employers. Examples include the following:

1. http://www.caritas.com
2. http://www.columbia.net
3. http://www.humana.com
4. http://www.phs.com

Web Bound Quarterly alone lists approximately one hundred separate potential major employers under the "Health Care Providers" subject heading.

A combination of traditional and on-line resume placement may provide the most thorough and effective approach to job hunting, as time permits. Also, the skills obtained in learning to job hunt electronically may enhance your future employability and provide contacts for subsequent networking and career development. Requesting e-mail addresses of prospective employers may provide an additional path to connect with transcription supervisors and keep in touch with the job market.

It should be mentioned that listing jobs on the World Wide Web is still a relatively new concept for medical transcription departments. Not all, or even most, available transcription positions will be listed on-line as of yet. With time, more and more positions may be posted this way.

Interacting with other on-line transcriptionists may also provide valuable contacts and information for pursuing the job search. On-line professionals may have valuable job hunting ideas to offer the novice. Joining either the medical transcription news group, sci.med.transcription, a topical message board or on-line forums such as America Online's medical transcription forum (keyword *medical transcription*) brings the job seeker into direct contact with working professional transcriptionists, who are often more than happy to share their experience and insight with newcomers. This electronic community expands the resources of the transcription student or new graduate. It also provides the opportunity to develop a network without leaving one's own living room. This is only one example of the potential of the Internet for connecting individuals and transferring valuable business information.

In addition to helping with job hunting, many medical and medical transcription Web sites provide relevant professional information to the working transcriptionist. Perhaps the most useful Web site for transcriptionists is the MT Daily site (http://www.mtdaily.com). This site contains extensive current information on transcription-related topics, as well as links to other transcription-related sites. Job openings and a resume-posting service are also included on this site.

There are also many medical Web sites of interest to transcriptionists. A good starting point to finding these is Medsearch (http://www.medsearch.com), which offers a wealth of medical information itself as well as a search engine dedicated to medical sites, and Medline, which performs searches of the National Library of Medicine database.

Other relevant medical and transcription sites include the following:

1. MT Desk (http://www.mtdesk.com), which includes an extensive list of transcription-related Web sites
2. Keeping Abreast of Medical Transcription (KAMT) (http://www.wwma.com/kamt)
3. Medical transcription forums on America Online (keyword *medical transcription*) and similar on-line services
4. MedicineNet (http://www.medicinenet.com)
5. Healthtouch (http://www.healthtouch.com)
6. Mayo Clinic (http://www.mayo.ivi.com)
7. CancerNet (http://www.icic.nci.nih.gov)
8. The Virtual Library (http://www.ohsu.edu/cliniweb/wwwvl)
9. Medical Matrix (http://www.slackinc.com/matrix)
10. The National Institutes of Health (http://www.nih.gov)
11. MT Universe (http://www.mtuniverse.com)

MT DAILY: AN ON-LINE NETWORKING RESOURCE

Mary Morken

MT Daily is a hub of activity for MTs at every stage of their career. Here are a few of the things you can do on this site:

You can find the e-mail address of over three thousand MTs and add yours to the state lists. You can find biographical sketches of MTs, telling how they found their first job. You can find lists of MT companies, company profiles, used books and equipment for sale, and jobs currently available, and you can post your resume.

You can search the whole site for a certain word or topic, using the search engine. You can post messages, contact MTs on your state message board, and read discussions on business, taxes, grammar, and ethical issues.

You can print jokes and find a list of Web sites published by individual MTs.

You can read about the latest developments in spell checkers, abbreviation expanders, voice file downloading, and transcription equipment. You can learn where there are book sales on medical word books, and you can get ideas for managing children while working at home.

You can chat with someone in the live chat room, travel a "Web ring" of MT Web sites, and find friends and mentors.

And you can meet me, the Web monitor. Let me invite you to become a part of the online MT community. Guides are far better than instruction books, and you will find lots of guides among your fellow MTs on-line. With the fast pace of technology and business changes ahead, we feel safe to be walking into the future together, because "all of us are smarter than one of us."

The many uses of the World Wide Web for medical transcriptionists may provide opportunities to expand the role and functions of the MT. Initially, the new transcriptionist may use the Web for job hunting, word lists, continuing education, and interaction with on-line colleagues. In time, the "on-line transcriptionist" may also develop skills in medical information retrieval and a growing familiarity with medical and allied health Web sites. This process could be developed as employers integrate on-line services with their transcription functions. That could eventually allow health care providers to have medical transcriptionists download relevant abstracts and articles from the Internet and append them to patients' charts.

However, as such a dramatic change, amounting to a rethinking of the transcriptionist's role, will not happen quickly, the individual transcriptionist may prefer to take the initiative. Independent medical research on the Web could supplement, or be used as a fall-back position, if technological changes or financial cutbacks curtail employment. Having the knowledge and skill to "mine" the Internet adds to the independent transcriptionist's portfolio.

It should also be remembered that the World Wide Web is still in its infancy, yet it already has over 100 million users worldwide. Each year will expand the numbers and complexity of the Web, creating new employment possibilities. Taking an active role on the Internet may be good insurance for continuing employability.

The Internet is a powerful growth opportunity for medical transcriptionists. Potentially, it provides a key not only to maintaining employment in changing times but also to advancing the medical transcriptionist's position for greater job satisfaction and compensation. Developing skills such as on-line searching and Web page design may also heighten the employability of the medical transcriptionist.

Not only health care providers but also many other individuals often need current, accurate medical information, both on technical and nontechnical levels. Those transcriptionists who can utilize the Internet to find that information can expand their occupational horizons.

REVIEW QUESTIONS

1. Name three general search engines on the World Wide Web.
2. What does the *http* in URLs stand for?
3. What is the correct Internet address of the MT Daily World Wide Web site?
4. What is an ISP?
5. Name three employment-related sites on the World Wide Web.
6. What does KAMT stand for?

RELATED WEB SITES

MULTILEVEL SEARCH ENGINES: http://www.freeality.com, http://www.metacrawler.com, http://www.go2net.com, http://www.mediconsult.com

PHARMACOLOGICAL DATA: http://www. pharminfo.com/pharmin.html

16
Advanced Technologies

LEARNING OBJECTIVES

- List factors driving requirements for increased productivity
- Discuss several types of macros and their uses
- Explain the two different types of voice-recognition software
- Explain the system requirements for running continuous voice-recognition programs

ON-THE-JOB PROFILE
Advancing Technology

I'm writing this in my home on a Pentium computer with 16 megabytes (MB) of random-access memory (RAM), using Microsoft Word word processing software. I haven't always had it so good. My first home computer, seven years ago, had only 256 kilobytes (K), or less than 1 MB, of RAM. It also lacked a hard drive and a printer. It was very, very slow at loading programs—often the number 50 would come on-screen and count backwards to 0 while loading. It would not have been possible to run a successful home transcription business with such limited equipment.

Today's computer hardware and software, less than a decade later, is amazing by comparison. Speeds as high as 450 megahertz (MHz) are currently available, with RAM up to 128 MB. Yet, while lecturing, I am often asked the questions, "How much computer do I really need to work at home? How much money should I expect to pay?"

There are two ways to answer these questions. One is to give the minimum, or lowball, estimate. Many transcription departments still use the older Word-Perfect 5.1 software because it is simple and very fast. This program lacks the graphics of more sophisticated programs, but it definitely gets the job done. You could even run it successfully on an old 486 computer, which means you could probably get an entire system for under $500.

ON-THE-JOB PROFILE   (continued)

I don't recommend that, however.

Instead, I recommend investing in the best possible equipment that you can afford. It's not enough to live for today and hope the future doesn't change things. Changes will happen, and technology will almost certainly continue to "up the ante."

A good example is continuous voice-recognition software. This wonderful and complex program requires a minimum of 32 MB of RAM to operate; 64 to 128 MB would be preferred. Home-based transcriptionists with older equipment don't even have the option of using it. Within the next few years there will probably be additional programs to enhance transcription. These will require even more sophisticated hardware. Those lagging in technology will be unable to stay in business.

Computer hard drives and computer games are also good indicators of impending changes. My first hard drive, in 1992, held 20 MB of information. Today my three-year-old drive holds 1,000 MB (1 gigabyte) and is bursting at the seams. When I started playing computer games, they took up about 512 K (half a megabyte). Today games can take up several hundred MB of hard drive, and some even offer "stripped-down" versions to load on laptops or older computers.

Technology reminds me of the ancient search for a perpetual motion machine. That never worked—and getting more advanced technology without paying the price for it will never work. A $2,000 computer system may seem beyond your means—but if it helps you earn another $10,000 a year by raising your production, then it becomes an investment you almost have to make. Inevitable advances in technology are changing and driving the global economy. Even in a quiet business like medical transcription, we need to keep up or risk being left behind.

The rapid development of computer hardware and software, as well as related technologies, may change the process and perhaps the very nature of medical transcription. Anyone currently entering the field, as well as those already professionally employed in it, should be aware of the potential consequences of these changes.

Medical transcriptionists are under increasing pressure to augment their production, and this is expected to continue for several reasons. Advances in technology allow enhanced production. Simultaneously, budgetary constraints require transcription supervisors to cut costs by maximizing production. The result is a "need for speed" that goes beyond a normal, relaxed typing pace. In years past, increased production was accomplished by upgrading from manual to electric typewriters, then to electronic typewriters, and finally to word processors. Using macros, or typing shortcuts, in word processing programs could significantly increase production. Also, the ability to edit and proofread a document before printing it out was a significant advantage over typing.

In the 1990s, ever more sophisticated microcomputers, such as those based on Intel's Pentium chip, have allowed the introduction of more powerful programs such as "expanders" and voice-recognition software. These technologies may allow the skilled transcriptionist to further increase production. However, they should be carefully considered prior to adoption, as every new process may have intrinsic drawbacks as well as benefits.

VOICE-RECOGNITION TECHNOLOGY

Edward S. Rosenthal, C.E.O., Next Generation Technologies, Inc.

Voice-recognition technologies have been available in a practical way since the mid-1970s. Early voice-recognition machines generally consisted of hardware-based computer systems with limited vocabularies, primarily capable of "command and control" functions. Command and control capability allowed the user to input commands and have the computer respond. These early machines also enabled a very limited use of "discrete speech" textual input.

By the early 1990s we saw the introduction of the first "software only" voice-recognition programs. This technological breakthrough was driven by development of sophisticated algorithms (Markov models) and advances in computer hardware.

Had voice-recognition technology not advanced beyond discrete speech and command and control software, it would have had only a small but faithful following. In early 1997, though, Dragon Systems of Newton, Massachusetts, introduced the first commercially available "continuous speech" voice-recognition software, called NaturallySpeaking. This single-user, single-topic software provided the ability to input text in a fairly natural style of speaking, with a reasonably high (95 percent) degree of accuracy. Shortly afterward, IBM released its product in the category, called ViaVoice. These programs represented a dramatic change in the capability of this technology and created the opportunity for widespread use of voice input into computer systems.

Since this introduction, the "engines" have become far more sophisticated, performing to a level of 98.5 percent accuracy in trials. They have a throughput rate of 160 words per minute. Voice-recognition technology is emerging as a practical way for people to create documents and generally interact with their PCs. Since the medical marketplace is not homogeneous, models for the implementation of voice-recognition technology will be as varied as the number of doctors, clinics, and hospitals practicing medicine.

In its current form, voice-recognition technology requires initialization by the user. Each user generally requires 30–120 minutes of reading to "teach" the computer how that person's voice sounds. The software is also context sensitive and uses linguistic content to generate the most accurate rendering in any given situation. Voice-recognition software should be "trained," using the type of

VOICE-RECOGNITION TECHNOLOGY   (continued)

language that will ultimately be used in a professional capacity, such as medical transcription.

Just as the computer mouse did not replace the keyboard, voice recognition is not intended to replace either of these devices. Many transcriptionists using voice-recognition software still use their familiar keystroke macro commands. This also means transcriptionists can keyboard until wrist or arm fatigue sets in, then open the microphone and begin "speaking in" text—or vice versa.

From an entrepreneurial standpoint, the use of voice-recognition technology and the electronic transmission of .WAV (sound) files creates the opportunity for increased efficiency, which means increased profitability. Two challenges facing medical transcription today are keeping up with changing technologies and finding the funding to stay current with computer hardware, software, and peripheral devices. Although funding current hardware may present difficulties, failure to make this investment may threaten the very existence of the practitioner or organization. Transcriptionists investing in knowledge and equipment create their own opportunities for profitability and personal fulfillment. They also create the opportunity to take advantage of future shifts in technology, by becoming accustomed to and managing change.

Macros are shortcuts built into word processing programs. The Microsoft Word program defines a macro as a series of word processing commands grouped together into a single command. There are several major categories into which the medical transcriptionist can group macros. The most obvious group is medical macros, such as typing *CHF* to get "congestive heart failure" (after typing the key that launches the macro, which is often the *Ctrl* or *Alt* key). This type of macro is very useful, particularly for long disease names and procedures such as "gastroesophageal reflux disease" or "coronary artery bypass grafting."

Of equal value, although perhaps less obvious, are macros for frequently repeated nontechnical or conversational phrases and figures of speech. Examples include *ITMT* for "in the meantime"; *PLEAS* for "We had the pleasure of seeing your patient in the clinic"; and *AYK* for "As you know, the patient is a ___-year-old man with a history of ____." Combining medical and conversational macros skillfully can reduce your keystrokes and raise your output.

Any good book of medical abbreviations can be scanned for medical macro ideas. For conversational macros, on-the-job familiarity, by listening to the speech patterns of regular dictators, is the best source.

A third category of macros is the format macros, such as one for a history and physical exam that includes the major headings, with physical exam subtext included. The accompanying box shows an example.

EXAMPLE : MACRO-GENERATED HISTORY AND PHYSICAL EXAMINATION REPORT FORM

CHIEF COMPLAINT/HISTORY OF PRESENT ILLNESS:

PAST MEDICAL HISTORY:

MEDICATIONS:

ALLERGIES:

FAMILY HISTORY:

SOCIAL HISTORY:

HABITS:

PHYSICAL EXAMINATION

VITAL SIGNS: Blood pressure _____, pulse _____, temperature _____, respirations _____. GENERAL: The patient is alert and oriented times three. HEAD: Normocephalic, atraumatic. Pupils are equal, round, and reactive to light and accommodation. NECK: Supple without adenopathy. CHEST: Clear to auscultation bilaterally. HEART: Regular rate and rhythm; no murmurs, rubs, or gallops. ABDOMEN: Soft, nontender, nondistended, with no hepatospleno-megaly. EXTREMITIES: Nontender to palpation, no edema.

LABORATORIES:

ASSESSMENT:
   1.
   2.
   3.

PLAN:
   1.
   2.
   3.

This form can be expanded or contracted as appropriate to the individual department's stylistic requirements and dictators' individual styles. Maintaining format macros for standard report forms, such as H&Ps and operative reports, can save time and repetition.

Finally, more extensive, "boilerplate" macros are indicated for reports on routine or specialized procedures that are frequently described by a particular care provider (or by a group of providers in a similar manner). These could include reports on such standard procedures such as botulin toxin injections, cataract surgery, and Moh's dermatologic surgery as well as specialty reports such as for amniocentesis. The boilerplate macro contains the entire text of a report, with blanks to be filled in (such as the patient's name, or husband's name and history) from dictation. If material from boilerplate macros is fully credited to a transcriptionist's line count, daily production quotas may be more easily met. Such macros also allow the transcriptionist to produce a greater output, thereby improving turnaround time.

The next technological step beyond the word processing macro is an "expander" program, more properly called word expansion and production software. Common expander programs for IBM-compatible computers include Abbreviate!, Flash Forward, Instant Text, MedPen, and Smartype Speedtyping. These programs combine the natural alertness and ability of the transcriptionist with built-in medical vocabularies and shortcuts. For example, typing the "first and last" letters *l* and *y* in Smartype will produce the word *lymphadenopathy* on the black "Smartline" onscreen. If that is the desired word, pressing the spacebar once will insert *lymphadenopathy* into the text. Several other choices, such as *lymph, lymphoma, lymphocytes,* and so on, will be presented as well, below the Smartline. These alternate choices are numbered for easy retrieval into the document if desired.

The goal of expansion programs is to anticipate necessary terminology and reduce the number of keystrokes needed to obtain it. Obviously, a certain amount of practice will be required to adapt to the technical requirements—and additional visual distraction—of a new expander program. However, particularly for those whose pay is based on production or can earn additional incentive pay, the opportunity to enhance income and also be more productive merits serious consideration.

Most major expansion software companies have World Wide Web sites where additional information can be obtained. These sites include the following:

http://www.med-pen.com
http://www.abbreviate.com
http://smartype.bhcom.com
http://walberg.com/summit.flash.html
http://twsolutions.com

Understandably, individual productivity gains will vary with any expansion software program. At the same time, maintaining their employability, as well as organizational and personal profitability, requires medical transcriptionists to keep up with and utilize technological innovations.

A 10 percent increase in productivity, from a 120-lines-per-hour base, would translate into approximately 500 lines per full-time week, or 25,000 additional lines per year per transcriptionist. On a productivity-oriented, 10-cents-per-line basis, that would be an additional $2,500 in gross annual income—not to mention the additional productivity benefit for the client or employer.

In addition to expansion software programs, much has been said about the introduction of voice-recognition software. Many working transcriptionists have expressed concerns about how this new technology will affect their jobs and whether it will ultimately eliminate them. As with all technological changes, reviewing the current status, future potential, and potential limitations of voice-recognition software is indicated to fully understand its impact.

Presently, there are two types of voice-recognition software available: "discrete" voice-recognition programs and "continuous" voice-recognition programs. Discrete voice recognition is the earlier version, designed to recognize words spoken with a brief pause between each word. In addition to words, punctuation must also be spoken. A brief "learning" session is often required for the program to recognize an individual's voice and make a "voice print" of it. The primary advantage of discrete voice recognition to an independent transcriptionist is its ability to run on computers as slow as 100 MHz and with only 16 MB of RAM. However, because of the necessary pauses between words, as well as the computer's occasional fallibility in recognizing spoken words, discrete voice-recognition software does not give a production advantage when compared to a professional transcriptionist's typing speed, and its value may be limited.

Continuous speech recognition, used in programs such as NaturallySpeaking (from Dragon Systems, Inc.), a widely available speech-recognition program, may meet or exceed the typing ability of the medical transcriptionist. The normal rate of speech, though varying among speakers, is estimated at two hundred to three hundred words per minute, versus approximately one hundred words per minute for a rapid typist. If continuous voice recognition can match or nearly match the rate of speech, this could present a significant potential for enhancing transcription productivity.

Minimum system requirements for NaturallySpeaking are a 133 MHz Pentium computer running the Windows 95, 98, or Windows NT operating system, at least 32 MB of RAM for Windows 95 or 98, or 48 MB for Windows NT, 60 MB of free hard disk space, a standard sound card, a CD-ROM drive, and a microphone. A faster computer, at least 200 MHz, and 64 or 128 MB of RAM is advisable. These system requirements may necessitate system upgrades or even new computer purchases for independent transcriptionists; however, the overall productivity advancement, if achieved, should compensate for the initial expense. Understandably, transcriptionists with less powerful home computer systems may be wary of such significant investment in a relatively new technology.

To use voice-recognition software for transcription, the transcriptionist listens to medical dictation (using headphones) and repeats it, word for word, into a microphone, allowing the computer to recognize it and "type" it on the screen. Thus the transcriptionist becomes more of a translator than a typist. Unusual words can be spelled as well as spoken, and there are also numerous editing commands.

The NaturallySpeaking system claims that above 95 percent accuracy can be achieved for general dictation. Additional vocabulary specific to medical terminology is available, at additional cost. However, as voice recognition becomes more widely adopted, the long-term health effects of "continuous talking" may require study. A combination of regular transcribing and talking may be preferred by full-time users.

Although voice-recognition technology is now viable and may free the transcriptionist from eight hours a day of typing, the knowledge and attentiveness of the medical transcriptionist is by no means unnecessary. A level of 95 percent accuracy is 5 percent too low for the medical transcriptionist—nor does medical dictation always run a straight and logical course. Often health care providers require insertions, deletions, or changes in previous paragraphs as further data becomes available. These changes, combined with regional and nonnative speaker accents, background noises, variability in dictation tone and volume, and individual dictation styles require the analytical abilities of the medical transcriptionist.

Medical terminology is constantly growing and evolving, and the American population is growing and aging. The increasing volume and complexity of medical reports suggests a long-term demand for the skill and accuracy of the medical transcriptionist, whatever the method employed to transcribe. Voice-recognition software can be a valuable tool for transcriptionists, but it is not a replacement for their abilities, judgment, and knowledge.

REVIEW QUESTIONS

1. What is the definition of a macro?
2. What is a format macro?
3. How could financial pressure, such as budget cutting, affect a transcription department's productivity standards?
4. Name three common expander programs.
5. How does the normal rate of speech compare to a normal professional typing speed?
6. How much RAM memory is the minimum requirement for continuous voice-recognition software?

RELATED WEB SITES

SPEECH RECOGNITION FOR MEDICAL TRANSCRIPTIONISTS: http://www.mtmeetingplace.com

INFORMATION ABOUT MACROS: http://www.deturi.com

MEDICAL VOICE RECOGNITION SOFTWARE: http://www.pacificvoice.com/products.htm

SPEECH RECOGNITION UPDATE JOURNAL: http://www.tmaa.com

17
The Future of Medical Transcription

LEARNING OBJECTIVES

- List five relevant trends that might affect the future of medical transcription
- Discuss aging and other demographic features of the U.S. population
- Explain economic influences expected to affect health care delivery and transcription departments
- Discuss reasons behind the trend toward self-employment
- Explain how the Internet will affect medical transcription

ON-THE-JOB PROFILE
Looking Ahead

The date is June 2, 2010. I adjust my cellular earphone for the first report. The dictator, a nursing assessment specialist, says:

First dictation, patient data in system. Standard code 14A, right shoulder pain. Please include phrase "range of motion limited beyond clinical indications" at end of second paragraph. Also, retrieve data on shoulder injuries, 2007–2010, Harbor Hospital database for the statistical page in the chart. Download three most relevant shoulder articles from Medscape Web site, current year, and attach. Then run a pharmaceutical search for rheumatoid arthritis meds and send to Rehab under separate cover.

Oh—could you go back to paragraph 1 in the standard and delete the word *etiology*? I think it was *etiology*. Well—never mind f it's not there, and have a nice day!

I speak in "standard 14A" with our voice-recognition software and add the individual message. Then I pull up the Injuries file, select "right shoulder," and zap in the desired stats. I split my screen for side-by-side word processor and Web site display on my 19-inch postdigital monitor. I select "shoulder articles," wishing

Although it is not possible to predict specific events, overall trends in business and health care can be identified and extrapolated to suggest future outcomes. Medical transcription, a specific occupation, is also a component of health care delivery and, on a larger scale, of the American and global economies, and trends in these larger areas will inevitably affect transcription as well.

Relevant trends that warrant discussion in considering the future of medical transcription include demographics, cost cutting and downsizing in business, home-based employment and self-employment, technological innovations, and the growth of the Internet.

DEMOGRAPHICS

In the United States, the population is growing by approximately 2 percent per year, based on a combination of greater births than deaths and extensive legal and illegal immigration. This amounts to roughly four million new persons each year, expanding the customer base of those needing medical records. Additionally, the large "baby boom" segment of the American population is aging (they are now in their forties and fifties) and will require increased health care services as they mature.

A related change is the widespread switch in the last decade from inpatient to outpatient services. This has reduced hospital inpatient reports but greatly expanded outpatient reports. Physicians are also more inclined to use allied health services (such as physical, occupational, speech, and vocational therapists). Nurse practitioners and physicians' assistants are also involved in dictation. With the increasing and aging population and the broader array of available health care services, the amount of work for medical transcriptionists seems likely to continue growing. Not only may the workload increase, it may also diversify with the corresponding increasing variety of health care providers. Medical terminology, equipment, treatments, and medications will continue to expand. Therefore the need for highly skilled, multispecialty medical transcriptionists may exceed the supply for some time.

The world's population, like that of the United States, is also increasing. Countries in the process of industrializing will need ever more access to health care and accurate medical records. Transcriptionists fluent in more than one language could be of great value in the global marketplace. Technological advances will allow work to be completed in one country and electronically delivered to recipients elsewhere. The global marketplace will change the health care industry in many ways.

COST CUTTING AND DOWNSIZING

In the last decade, economics has played an increasingly significant role in health care delivery. This financial pressure is expected to continue. Although medical transcriptionists have not had the visibility of physicians or managers when cost cutting has occurred, it is expected that all aspects of health care costs will be closely scrutinized from now on. For the medical transcriptionist this may mean additional production pressure, as supervisors will be required to obtain maximal output per employee. On a day-to-day level, this could mean vacant positions might not be filled promptly, with current employees expected to pick up the slack, or new positions might not be created. It could also mean that turnaround times will decrease due to inadequate staffing, with subsequent dissatisfaction on the part of health care providers. "The bottom line" will no longer be an abstract concept to transcriptionists but a very real reminder that customer satisfaction is vital to maintaining everyone's employment. Transcriptionists will be challenged by higher productivity and accuracy standards but may not receive the technological support to comfortably achieve higher output goals.

HOME-BASED EMPLOYMENT

In our increasingly urban society, working at home presents more and more advantages over commuting in regard to the time, expense, and risks associated with traveling to work. Time spent commuting to the work site may be better spent in home-based productivity. The cost of operating a vehicle may be substantially reduced by eliminating work-related travel. Similarly, food costs for meals at home will be lower, and the need for an extensive professional wardrobe will decline.

With multiple financial incentives and the potential to spend increased time with children and other family members, a strong continuing trend toward home employment is anticipated. For the medical transcriptionist, if the work-at-home option is possible through an employer, a digital dictation system may be installed in the home. For the self-employed transcriptionist, tapes or re-recording equipment may be used to work independently, with the probability of declining prices for digital dictation systems in the near future.

Despite the complexity of self-employment in terms of taxes, record keeping, and marketing, the psychological benefits of being your own boss are substantial for many persons. With advances in personal computer technology allowing comparable productivity from a home-based business as from an on-site transcriptionist, medical transcriptionists have an opportunity to take greater control of their work life. As technological advances continue, this option will probably expand. Similarly, as employers recognize that home-based employees may be less costly and more productive than on-site employees, economic necessities should prevail in placing medical transcriptionists more and more in the home setting.

TECHNOLOGICAL INNOVATIONS

Forthcoming technical innovations will probably include development and refinement of existing technologies (such as voice-recognition software, expander programs, and word processing programs) as well as new and unexpected "quantum" innovations not predictable by extrapolating from current systems. Inevitable refinements in telecommunications, based on installation of fiber optic cable, will increase the basic speed of communications. At the same time, increased demand on phone lines and high-speed transmission lines will strain new and existing systems even after they are upgraded. The typical home, formerly equipped with only a single telephone line, may now require two or more lines with at least one high-speed ISDN line—and have a cellular phone and pager as well. These amenities, just as home computers are now, will become taken for granted as they are adopted and incorporated into the American lifestyle.

Advanced technologies may be integrated into transcription software packages, allowing the user to employ word processing, voice recognition, and Internet access in a seamless system. Just as physicians have moved from basic patient care to more diversified "managed" care, medical transcriptionists may move beyond basic word processing and have a variety of tools from which to choose to accomplish their task. A medical transcriptionist 10 years from now may need to be skilled in using multiple computer systems, both local and network, and electronic medical records may incorporate Web site links as a matter of course.

INTERNET GROWTH

Students of history will recall that beginning in the 1700s the Industrial Revolution brought significant, even radical changes to European society and ultimately the world. Similarly, the rise of mass production in the early 20th century transformed our national economy and eventually provided the catalyst for the development of today's global economy.

It is quite possible that the combination of widespread personal computer ownership and 24-hour, worldwide Internet access may have a similarly powerful effect, as more and more persons link together across national and international boundaries. Never before in human history has so much information been accessible to the average person in the home. Never before have so many millions of people had the potential to interact easily across cultural and national lines. As global Internet access grows, the opportunities for commerce and information sharing will be enormous.

Medical transcription, like any other computer-related business, will feel the effects of this revolution. As health care providers recognize the wealth of information available on the Web and the many ways it may be used to improve patient care and expand medical records, transcriptionists may be called on to use the Internet as a normal facet of their jobs. Those able to make this transition may find almost unlimited opportunities for managing and processing health-related information.

 ON-THE-JOB PROFILE
Trends

When I started working for the University of Washington transcription department three years ago, we had about 40 transcriptionists, one-third of whom worked at home as telecommuters. As of this writing, over one-half work at home. I would not be surprised if our office were closed in the next few years, with all the transcriptionists telecommuting. In our area, many hospitals have already taken this step. This, to me, represents a trend.

Anticipating trends helps workers, including medical transcriptionists, be prepared for—or even avoid—unpleasant surprises. Those who prefer the social interaction that comes with working in an office may have to prepare for fewer choices along those lines. Home workers tend to be more productive than office workers, and employers are able to transfer "overhead" costs, such as rent and electricity, to them. Therefore it makes more financial sense to employ telecommuters than to keep up a costly office. When budgetary pressures increase, this choice may become a necessity.

Likewise, the trend toward technological enhancements has momentum and will be difficult to challenge. Just as cost control favors telecommuting, cost efficiency demands increased production from each individual transcriptionist. If software such as word expansion and voice-recognition programs can routinely increase production, these will become necessities in the long run.

In the late 1980s I worked for a clinic that was just starting to implement word processors instead of typewriters. This was a new technology to our workers, adopted to increase our productivity and flexibility in revising documents. I specifically remember that one of our transcriptionists just "could not get it." She had done fine with a typewriter, but could not grasp the concept of working on a computer monitor, proofreading on the screen, and printing a report out after her entire document was done rather than letter by letter. She tried hard, as this was her livelihood, but she could not do it. As you might expect, the clinic did not keep a typewriter just for her convenience, and she was eventually let go. She could not adjust to the trend.

Another trend likely to affect our profession is speed. Transcribed documents can now be transmitted electronically to dictators as soon as they are com-

ON-THE-JOB PROFILE   (continued)

pleted, and reviewed on screen immediately. This immediacy may raise expectations of instant service, and once adopted it will become the norm. This may have an impact on expectations regarding transcribing time. For example, I was recently given a "stat" report with 40 minutes of dictation—about 2–3 hours of transcribing time—and asked to complete it in one hour. Once customers get used to instant delivery, they may expect instant transcription.

Whatever trends influence the future, transcriptionists, like all other workers, must continue to adapt to continue being employed. At the same time, they must also insist on reasonable expectations and adequate time to complete documents accurately. The importance of accurate medical records cannot be overridden by a desire for haste and cost cutting. Our patients will always deserve quality as much as quantity.

REVIEW QUESTIONS

1. Why will the aging of the "baby boomers" affect health care delivery?
2. How could future cost cutting affect medical transcription departments?
3. Will the trend toward working at home likely continue or decline? For what reasons?
4. Why is self-employment more complex than working as an employee?
5. What is a hypertext link? Why will the Internet be increasingly important to medical transcriptionists?
6. What are your personal predictions for the future of medical transcription?

RELATED WEB SITES

FUTUREFILE TRENDS WEB SITE: http://www.futurefile.com
SCIENCE OF FUTURISM: http://www.alumni.gatech.edu/news/alummag/sum93/sci.html
FUTURE HEALTH TEXT: http://www.ipli.com/th-book.htm

Answers to Review Questions

CHAPTER 1

1. The medical transcription profession has diversified in the last five years, with advancing technology allowing more transcriptionists to work at home, either as telecommuters or independent contractors. Also, technologies such as word expansion software and voice-recognition software have increased production, thereby increasing earning potential.

2. The types of training available to become a medical transcriptionist include community college and technical college courses, correspondence courses, mentoring by a medical transcriptionist, and distance learning via the Internet.

3. The Myers Briggs Type Indicator identifies psychological traits such as introversion or extroversion, sensing or intuitive personalities, thinking or feeling personalities, and judging or perceiving personalities.

4. The local job market could be evaluated by studying newspapers and local health-related publications, consulting local job lines and human resource bulletin boards at health care facilities, attending local AAMT meetings, and researching local jobs at state employment offices and public libraries.

CHAPTER 2

1. Three important characteristics of a positive work space are adequate lighting, good air quality, and ergonomically sound chairs and workstations.

2. Transcription wages are generally lower in rural areas than in urban areas.

3. Transcribing for a clinic could be different from transcribing for a hospital because some reports might be less difficult, fewer "stat" reports might be required, and the overall knowledge and experience needed by the transcriptionist might be less.

4. A job hunt scrapbook can provide lists of employers who hire medical transcriptionists, job requirements, shifts available, and contact persons.

5. A reasonable production standard for a medical transcriptionist might be 100 to 150 lines per hour average on basic word processing equipment (without word expansion software or voice-recognition software).

6. A reasonable quality standard would be 97 percent or above. Continuous quality improvement is always desirable.

CHAPTER 3

1. "In-house" medical transcription positions can sometimes be identified by human resources bulletin boards at health care facilities.

2. Tests that may be required in addition to a transcribing test include spelling, editing, medical abbreviations, and proofreading tests.

3. The best preparation for a personal interview includes getting a good night's sleep, researching the individual facility, practicing good hygiene and wearing professional attire, and allowing adequate travel time to the interview site.

4. A follow-up letter of thanks should be written within 48 hours of a job interview.

5. In a transcription test, accuracy is essential; speed is desirable, of course, but can be developed over time.

6. Contact phone numbers of previous employers are convenient for the prospective employer and should be included on the job application.

CHAPTER 4

1. The purpose of a trial offer is to demonstrate proficiency in the absence of actual transcription experience.

2. "Piggybacking" refers to building a network of contacts among fellow job hunters to share job search information.

3. A transcriptionist should have one or two years of office transcription experience before pursuing full self-employment, unless he or she has already been self-employed in another field, in which case six months to one year of transcribing may suffice.

4. A transcription internship allows both staff and intern to get acquainted in a real work setting, evaluate one another, and develop a positive working relationship.

5. A lateral transfer is a two-step process that involves obtaining employment in a related department, such as medical records, and then transferring into medical transcription.

6. Preparing for a job fair includes making multiple copies of one's resume, researching attending companies, wearing professional business attire, and bringing a notebook to track contacts and job opportunities.

CHAPTER 5

1. Knowledge of different word processing systems is valuable to employers because different transcription departments use different systems, and they may also change or upgrade systems periodically.

2. More than one person should proofread a resume, both for typographical errors and for stylistic improvements.

3. An on-line resume is a resume that has been posted on the World Wide Web. Such a resume is accessible by potential employers all over the world.

4. Skills worth mentioning in a cover letter include word processing skills, computer skills, the ability to type fast, knowledge of an alternate language, and English language editing skills. An applicant should also mention any work-related distinctions or honors he or she has attained.

5. A follow-up letter might be preferable to an unscheduled visit or call because medical transcription departments and department supervisors are generally very busy.

CHAPTER 6

1. Techniques to overcome a low salary offer include mentioning a previous higher salary, explaining the need for a higher salary due to rising costs of living, and offering to accept a temporary compromise wage with a three-month review guaranteed.

2. The level of benefits adds greatly to the base salary offered, considering the cost of medical and dental insurance and the value of sick days, vacation pay, and similar benefits.

3. Negotiation of benefits or salary should not be casually undertaken, as there is always a chance of losing a possible job offer in an inflexible situation.

4. A new hire should keep and carefully file all relevant documentation related to his or her employment, such as contracts, employee manuals, written job descriptions, tax records, and benefits summaries.

5. An unacceptably low wage lessens future earnings, because most raises are calculated as a percentage of one's current salary.

6. The hidden costs of benefits to employees include payroll deductions for partial payment of medical and dental insurance premiums, out-of-pocket co-pays for clinic visits, and deductions for mandatory retirement plans.

CHAPTER 7

1. "The wall" is the point in an unsuccessful job hunt (generally after three months of searching) when it seems unlikely that the job seeker will find a job. When a job seeker "hits the wall," he or she must consider other strategies and options.

2. Three factors that might prevent a job seeker from landing a transcription job are incompatible scheduling, a lack of local contacts, and simply not being suitable for a career as a medical transcriptionist.

3. Personal factors that could adversely affect employability include child care requirements that conflict with work schedules, an inability or unwillingness to work weekends or evenings if required, or an inability to work full-time.

4. Personal factors that indicate suitability for a medical transcription position include excellent language skills, knowledge of multiple word processing systems, excellent interpersonal skills, knowledge of medical terminology, and familiarity with basic medical procedures.

5. How to adjust an unsuccessful job search is an individual decision. Possible changes include increasing the time and effort expended in job hunting, adopting a more positive attitude, making greater use of interpersonal contacts among health care professionals, and researching local job availability again, in greater detail.

CHAPTER 8

1. A boilerplate macro is a macro that produces an entire preformatted report. They are particularly useful for reports on procedures that vary little from patient to patient or otherwise contain a lot of standard information.

2. A transcriptionist could reject an assigned job because he or she lacked adequate time to complete the report before the end of his or her shift.

3. Transcriptionists use medical references on a daily basis to look up unfamiliar terms, check correct capitalization and style, and reinforce their existing knowledge base.

4. Drug reference books vary in terms of their ease of use. Transcriptionists should study them ahead of time, before they need them, to familiarize themselves with how each such reference is organized and the type of information it contains.

5. Directing work flow is a management function, probably handled by the transcription supervisor or delegated to the lead transcriptionist.

6. A written job description is necessary for a medical transcriptionist. This can indicate specific duties and responsibilities, employer expectations, and standards for productivity and accuracy.

CHAPTER 9

1. Two valuable functions of macros are improving accuracy and increasing production, by reducing the number of keystrokes necessary to produce reports.

2. Many World Wide Web sites now provide transcription information. MT Daily and MT Desk are two well-known examples.

3. Three items that indicate professional development are joining AAMT, networking with local medical transcriptionists, and becoming certified as a medical transcriptionist by an official certifying body.

4. Four technological development items are learning new word processing software, improving home computer skills, developing Internet searching skills, and adopting advanced technologies as they arise.

CHAPTER 10

1. The best technique for locating unfamiliar words in a medical reference book is cross-referencing.
2. Correcting on the fly means correcting mistakes while typing; this is done in addition to performing a final proofread and spell check, not in place of them.
3. Familiarity with names of health care providers can be hastened by periodically reviewing dictator names and by writing down unusual name spellings.
4. The three steps of high-quality proofreading are correcting while transcribing, careful final proofreading, and spell checking each document.
5. Three tips for better critical listening are listening to what is dictated rather than anticipating familiar phrases, focusing on the spoken word rather than on background noises, and identifying the initial letter of difficult words to help identify them.

CHAPTER 11

1. Organizational isolation may adversely affect medical transcriptionists by keeping them "out of the loop," unfamiliar with organizational changes and opportunities.
2. Incentive pay is pay given for production and/or accuracy above a certain standard, in addition to one's regular wages.
3. The two major presenting symptoms of carpal tunnel syndrome are numbness and tingling in the wrists and hands.
4. Some medical transcriptionists are paid on a production basis, with or without benefits, depending on their contract.
5. Weekend coverage is necessary in 365-day-a-year organizations such as hospitals, and the responsibility for providing this coverage may need to be shared by staff members on a rotation basis.

CHAPTER 12

1. The lead transcriptionist generally has more nonproductive time so he or she can perform support and coordinating duties, such as quality assurance, to assist the transcription supervisor.
2. The transcription supervisor plans for and adapts to changes in departmental workloads.
3. A medical transcription instructor generally teaches at a community college or technical college level.

4. A medical information specialist performs library and Internet research on health-related topics for individuals or organizations.

CHAPTER 13

1. Some employers supply computers and transcription systems for telecommuters, to maintain consistent standards of documentation and confidentiality.
2. Telecommuting is not an appropriate choice for every medical transcriptionist, as the relative social isolation and possible organizational isolation may not be in the best interest of all individuals.
3. A telecommuter should have an extensive medical reference library on hand, including medical dictionaries, formularies, and medical specialty references. Internet access for database searching is also highly recommended.
4. Internet access is strongly recommended for transcriptionists in general and telecommuters in particular. The current medical information available on the World Wide Web, including directories of health care providers, has great value and will continue to expand.
5. Telecommuting often increases productivity, possibly due to fewer social distractions and the familiarity and comfort of the home environment.
6. Regular contact with the transcription office will support continued knowledge of organizational needs and changes and maintain valuable personal relationships.

CHAPTER 14

1. Three economic advantages of working at home are lower transportation costs, lower food costs, and lower clothing costs.
2. Working at home is likely to increase productivity due to a more positive environment, familiar surroundings, incandescent rather than fluorescent lighting, and fewer distractions than in the workplace.
3. Working at home could lessen the chances of promotion, if access to key personnel and awareness of organizational needs are reduced.
4. Planning for future expansion of a home office allows a transcription business to grow and mature without having to relocate.
5. Three purchasing factors, with regard to price and value, are that prices for a unique item can vary, levels of quality can vary, and prices are intrinsically negotiable.
6. Timing may affect major office purchases if goods are purchased during times of low demand or overabundant supply.
7. Factors affecting fees charged by independent transcriptionists are the level of income required for profitability, customers' perception of fairness, and current community standards (fees set by competitors).

CHAPTER 15

1. General search engines on the World Wide Web include Yahoo!, AltaVista, Excite!, Hotbot, Infoseek, and Lycos.
2. The *http* in a URL stands for "hypertext transfer protocol."
3. The correct Internet address of the MT Daily World Wide Web site is http://www.mtdaily.com.
4. An ISP, or Internet service provider, is a company that provides dial-up access (by modem) to the Internet.
5. Employment-related sites on the World Wide Web include Jobbankusa, Jobquest, and Jobsmarts.
6. KAMT stands for Keeping Abreast of Medical Transcription, the name of a Web site for transcriptionists.

CHAPTER 16

1. A macro is a word processing shortcut that allows the user to call up a word, a phrase, or even an entire report by typing in just a few keystrokes. In Microsoft Word, the user can also create macros that perform a series of word processing commands.
2. A format macro is a macro that produces a frequently used report format, such as the format used for an operative note.
3. Budget cutting could affect a transcription department's production standards by decreasing the number of transcriptionists available to produce the required number of reports, necessitating higher output per transcriptionist to maintain turnaround times.
4. Commonly used expander programs for IBM-compatible computers include Abbreviate!, Smartype Speedtyping, Instant Text, Flash Forward, and MedPen.
5. The normal rate of speech (200 to 300 words per minute) is significantly faster than a normal professional typing speed of 80 to 100 words per minute.
6. The minimum RAM required for continuous voice-recognition software is 32 MB; 64 MB or more is preferred.

CHAPTER 17

1. The aging of the "baby boomers" may affect health care by requiring additional medical and home health care services to support a larger geriatric population.
2. Future cost cutting could affect medical transcription departments by reducing the number of transcriptionists, placing additional productivity requirements on them to meet turnaround times, or encouraging more outsourcing of transcription to private services.

3. The trend toward working at home, particularly in urban areas with high traffic congestion, is likely to continue.

4. Self-employment is more complex than employee status because of additional record-keeping and tax requirements, the necessity to procure and maintain business accounts and purchase supplies, and the need to manage production and ensure quality.

5. A hypertext link is a word or image on a Web page that, when clicked with a mouse, calls up another page, often on a separate Web site. The Internet will be increasingly important to medical transcriptionists as more and more medical information becomes available for research purposes and more telecommuters use the Internet to transmit data and reports.

6. Personal predictions for the future of medical transcription will vary with the individual student and the student's perception of social and technological changes likely to affect the field.

Bibliography

JOB SEARCHING

TAUNEE BESSON, *National Business Employment Weekly Cover Letters,* 2nd ed. (New York: Wiley, 1996).

PAT CRISCITO, *Resumes in Cyberspace* (Hauppauge, NY: Barron's, 1997).

MARCIA R. FOX AND PAT MORTON, *Job Search 101* (Indianapolis: JIST Works, 1997).

RAYMOND A. KEVANE, *Employment Power: Take Control of Your Career* (Seattle: Peanut Butter Publishing, 1994).

ADELE LEWIS AND GARY JOSEPH GRAPPO, *How to Write Better Resumes,* 4th ed. (Hauppauge, NY: Barron's, 1993).

MEDICAL TRANSCRIPTION

DONNA AVILA-WEIL AND MARY GLACCUM, *The Independent Medical Transcriptionist,* 2nd ed. (Windsor, CA: Rayve, 1994).

RACHELLE S. BLAKE, *Delmar's Medical Transcription Handbook,* 2nd ed. (Albany, NY: Delmar Publishers, 1998).

LINDA CAMPBELL, et al., *Medical Transcription: Fundamentals & Practice* (Englewood Cliffs, NJ: Health Professions Institute/Prentice Hall, 1994).

ROGER CRAWFORD, "The Bounce Factor: Six Springboards for Success," *Journal of the American Association for Medical Transcription* 17 (1998), no. 1, 29–30.

CLAUDIA TESSIER, *The AAMT Book of Style for Medical Transcription* (Modesto, CA: American Association for Medical Transcription, 1995).

CLAUDIA TESSIER, "What Will the Future Bring?" *Journal of the American Association for Medical Transcription* 17 (1998), no. 1, 4.

CAROL TICE, "Dangers for the Deskbound," *Today's Careers* 9 (1998), no. 23, 1–2.

LOUISE F. TIMMER, "A Medical Transcription Program That Really Works," *Journal of the American Association for Medical Transcription* 17 (1998), no. 3, 45–48.

CAREER AND FINANCIAL MANAGEMENT

HERMAN HOLTZ, *The Complete Work-At-Home Companion,* 2nd ed. (Rocklin, CA: Prima Publishing, 1994).

C. FREDERICK WIEGOLD, ed., *The Wall Street Journal Lifetime Guide to Money* (New York: Hyperion, 1997).

INTERNET

KIMBERLY ANDOSCA, "Search Engines on the Internet," *Journal of the American Association for Medical Transcription* 17 (1998), no. 2, 41–43.

ALFRED AND EMILY GLOSSBRENNER, *Making More Money on the Internet* (New York: McGraw-Hill, 1996).

ROBERT KILEY, *Medical Information on the Internet* (Edinburgh, Scotland: Churchill Livingstone, 1996).

JENNIFER MARTIN, "Putting the Internet to Work for You," *Journal of the American Association for Medical Transcription* 17 (1998), no. 3, 22–24.

MATTHEW NAYTHONS AND ANTHONY CATSIMATIDES, *The Internet Health, Fitness, & Medicine Yellow Pages.* (Berkeley, CA: Osborne/McGraw-Hill, 1995).

DAVID SACHS AND HENRY STAIR, *The 7 Keys to Effective Web Sites* (Upper Saddle River, NJ: Prentice Hall, 1997).

Web Bound Quarterly, entire Spring 1997 issue.

American Association for Medical Transcription presents:

A Medical Transcriptionist's Bill of Rights

Whereas, the medical transcriptionist contributes significantly to the delivery and quality of patient care, while also helping to assure appropriate reimbursement, promote research integrity, and fulfill providers' legal obligations through documentation of health services.

Be it therefore declared that each medical transcriptionist has the following rights:

I. **The right to an appropriate job classification** that reflects the expertise and responsibilities required of medical transcriptionists.

II. **The right to fair pay**, including overtime when paid by the hour or by production, with full disclosure of the basis on which pay is determined.

III. **The right to benefits**, including sick pay, holiday pay, vacation pay, and health insurance.

IV. **The right to nondiscrimination** on any basis, including sex, age, disability, race, religion, and ethnicity.

V. **The right to a safe work environment** that promotes prevention, identification, and treatment of work-related injuries and disabilities.

VI. **The right to communicate with others** in order to assist or be assisted, including feedback on performance and inquiries made regarding dictation or transcription.

VII. **The right to edit dictation** as necessary and appropriate to produce a clear, concise, and accurate document, correcting grammar, punctuation, and spelling, drawing attention to inaccuracies, inconsistencies, incomprehensible dictation, and potential risk management concerns.

VIII. **The right to professional resources** (print, video, audio, electronic) that facilitate the preparation of accurate and complete documents.

IX. **The right to environmental resources** (space, equipment, furniture, lighting, and supplies) that promote the efficient and effective accomplishment of responsibilities.

X. **The right to professional development and confirming education opportunities.**

XI. **The right to professional association membership and participation.**

XII. **The right to participate in the development of, to be informed of, and to adopt professional guidelines ar d standards** for medical transcription.

XIII. **The right to respect and recognition** as a professional, as a medical language specialist, and, for those who have earned the designation, as a certified medical transcriptionist (CMT).

XIV. **The right to participate fully as a healthcare professional in the preparation of patient care documentation** in order to enhance the quality of that documentation and thereby the quality of patient care.

© 1997 AAMT • PO Box 576187 • Modesto, CA 95357
Phone: 209-551-0883 • Fax: 209-551-9317
E-mail:aamt@sna.com • Web Site: http://www.aamt.org/aamt

Index